BEWARE
THE MIND
HUSTLER
IDENTIFYING SELF-DESTRUCTIVE THOUGHTS AND DISTRACTIONS

BEWARE
THE MIND
HUSTLER

IDENTIFYING SELF-DESTRUCTIVE THOUGHTS AND DISTRACTIONS

by:

DR. ALFONSO WYATT

Strategic Destiny
DESIGNING FUTURES THROUGH FAITH & FACTS

Beware The Mind Hustler: Identifying Self-Destructive Thoughts And Distractions

Copyright © 2019 by Dr. Alfonso Wyatt

All rights reserved. Except permitted under the U.S. Copyright Act of 1976, no part of this book may be used, reproduced, distributed or transmitted by in any form or by any means, graphic, electronic or mechanical or stored in a database or retrieval system, without the prior written permission to the publisher except in the case of brief quotations embodied in critical articles and reviews.

Strategic Destiny books may be purchased through booksellers or by sending an email to alfonsowyatt09@gmail.com.

Cataloging-in-Publication Data is on file with the Library of Congress.
Library of Congress Control Number: 2019914814
ISBN: 978-0-9982566-2-7 (paperback)
ISBN: 978-0-9982566-3-4 (digital)

Interior and Cover Design: Taneki Dacres of Vine Publishing, Inc. (vinepublish.com)

Printed in the United States of America.

DEDICATION

This book is dedicated to credible messengers across the country fighting to resist The Mind Hustler by mentoring, counseling, employing and encouraging teens and young adults to live free, grow and thrive. I am grateful for the example of my mother and father's servant leadership showing me at a young age the importance of helping people in need, especially brothers and sisters in and out of the prison system.

A special thanks to CC-FY staff and facilitators of the Credible Messenger Institute (CMI) and facilitators of the Institute for Transformative Mentoring (ITM); a special shout-out to all CMI and ITM students, as well as brothers and sisters who graciously shared their lived experience in writing in an effort to change and control their collective life narrative.

I send my appreciation to Kim Mayner for her superb editing work.

TABLE OF CONTENTS

Foreword	xi
Preface	xvii
First Ever Interview With The Mind Hustler	3
PART I: ESSAYS TMH DOES NOT WANT YOU TO READ	**7**
Free Your Mind	9
Functional Dysfunction	13
Transforming Trouble	17
Lost In Ruminationville	21
Stuck On Stuck	25
Death To Fear	29
Troubled Mind Games	33
The Other You In You	37
Anchored To A Cloud	43
Check Your Life-Bags	47
The Enemy Within	51
Family Hurt	55
Phoenix Rising	59
PART II: RESILIENCE, RESISTANCE, RESURRECTION	**63**
The Mind Hustler Exposed	65
The Mind Hustler, B Cincere Wilson	67

Fear Won't Stop Me, Khadijah Allen	71
Letter To The Mind Hustler, Jason Acosta	75
The Mind Hustler, Margarita Montgomery	79
The Mind Hustler, Jamel Massey	83
The Trickster, William Eric Waters	87
Letters That Heal, Jessica A. Maldonado	91
A Letter To My Young People, Perrian S. Glasby	95
Letter To The Mind Hustler, Ebony Walcott	97
Letter To The Mind Hustler, Bishop Darren Ferguson	99
Beware The Mind Hustler, Tyisha Jackson	101
Beware Mind Hustler, Keonn Sheppard	105
The Mind Hustler At Work, John Duckworth	109
Fire, Greiny Rodriguez	113
Beware The Mind Hustler, Sekou Shakur	117
My Search For Self, Todderick Brockington	121
Frenemies, G.S. Brooks	123

PART III: FORTIFY YOUR MIND IN YOUR OWN WORDS — 129

Seven Steps To Defeat The Mind Hustler	131
Go Back To The Future	137
Life Turning Point	139
Your Personal Letter To The Mind Hustler	141
The Power of One	143
The Last Word, Vivian D. Nixon	145

TABLE OF CONTENTS

PART IV: SUGGESTED READINGS   *151*

PART V: COMPILATION OF WISDOM SAYINGS   *157*

FOREWORD

No weapon against you is stronger than the worst version of yourself. That is the essential insight of this timely book. The Mind Hustler, or TMH, which sounds appropriately like a dangerous drug that can destroy you with your own cooperation. This does not mean that you do not face hardships that are not of your own making. We sometimes catch bad hands in the card game of life. That's how it goes. But that would only explain some of the trouble you face. The Mind Hustler translates explanations into excuses and enables you to fail completely. And as Reverend Wyatt informs us, The Mind Hustler does not rest. It ever lurks, probing for weakness, ready to pounce. Brother Wyatt's analysis, his useful metaphor, seems right to me. He reminds me (and I've known him for more than 60 years) that I have been in a long battle to operate in a positive way. I have been to the same edges to which some of you have journeyed. The story goes something like this.

Born in Harlem and growing up in Queens, I was a good student apparently on a good path. I had good people around me. I received a lot of good advice. But I also faced challenges in the streets and did not always meet them well. I succumbed to the heroin plague that swept through—got pushed through—town in the 1960s. I had thought of myself as a potential leader, but my main leadership move at that point was being the first person on my block to land in the Adolescent Remand Center on Rikers

Island. I don't know if that's still the name of the facility and, if so, if it is configured the same way it was back then. But if it is, that means that you can locate cell block 5, cell 5A6. That was my spot.

Fortunately, I did not stay long thanks to a fantastic aunt, decent lawyer, and a sympathetic judge. However, I had to struggle not to return. My basic ways did not change until I was shaken by some of the political events of the 1960s and 1970s. Some people I knew, and many I did not, were fighting to improve my neighborhood and neighborhoods like it. Some of these people put their lives on the line in fighting for social justice. Some lost their lives. Some were as young as 17. I was 18 and pretty much fighting for nothing that mattered. That had to change and did. I committed to becoming a positive change agent and eventually decided that the contribution that I was best suited to make was in the field of education. The accomplishments have not been easily attained. They never are. But all I needed was for them to be possible. I figured that with my mind right I could take care of the rest.

I am not saying that you have to become directly involved in progressive politics to ward off The Mind Hustler. That simply proved to be helpful for me. I am saying that you must fully believe in something far more strongly than you believe in what The Mind Hustler offers. That offer involves illicit gains, broken lives, and often prison. As you might imagine, I know a number of people who wished they had turned that offer down.

On occasion, I have taught in prison. When I was on the faculty of Syracuse University, I also taught African-American literature for a couple of semesters at Auburn Correctional Facility. I had one student who said he thought he knew me. I doubted him. I actually knew many folks in Auburn; some even called out to me the first time I crossed the yard headed to the classroom building. This caused the guard who escorted me to look at me with suspicion. I doubted this student knew me because he wasn't in my age group. Then he asked me if I ever worked in Brooklyn at Medgar Evers College. I responded that I had worked there, but I wondered how he knew that. It turns out that he had been a resident in a youth home across the street from the front entrance to the college and remembered my coming to work in the morning. He said he wished he had studied with me back then. I said, "me too." He had a very long sentence to serve.

I guess I have been drawn to campuses, prisons, and other sites because they have been places for me to both learn and teach. The people I have met, including the young man I mentioned above, have always helped me in my humble efforts to produce wisdom and understanding, even "overstanding." Knowledge comes from everywhere. If I have retained one thing so far, it is this: Experiences matter but how we respond to our experiences matters more. I am reminded of a poem by Portia Nelson titled, "Autobiography in Five Short Chapters":

Chapter I
I walk down the street.
There is a deep hole in the sidewalk.
I fall in.
I am lost...I am helpless.
It isn't my fault.
It takes forever to find a way out.

Chapter II
I walk down the same street.
There is a deep hole in the sidewalk.
I pretend I don't see it.
I fall in again.
I can't believe I am in this same place.
But it isn't my fault.
It still takes a long time to get out.

Chapter III
I walk down the same street.
There is a deep hole in the sidewalk.
I see it is there.
I still fall in…it's a habit…but,
my eyes are open.
I know where I am.
It is my fault.
I get out immediately.

Chapter IV
I walk down the same street.
There is a deep hole in the sidewalk.
I walk around it.

Chapter V
I walk down another street.

The other street is where Brother Wyatt is trying to take us. In these tumultuous times, in which the need for fresh and wise perspectives is pressing, this is a good move. This book should prove helpful in the cause.

-Keith Gilyard
Sparks Professor of English and African American Studies, Penn State

Keith Gilyard is a prominent writer and American professor of English who teaches and researches in the fields of rhetoric, composition, literacy studies, sociolinguistics, and African American literature. Interested in the complex interplay among race, ethnicity, language, writing, and politics, Gilyard's work investigates the differences between authentic student voice and the dominant discourse of the academy. His primary interest lies in identifying intersections of African American English and composition practices. Advocating African American English as a legitimate discourse, Gilyard is a prominent voice in the movement to recognize ethnic and cultural discourses other than Standard English as valid. As a literary scholar, his interests have been in the interplay between African American literature and rhetorical criticism and in bio-critical work.

Gilyard received his Bachelor of Science degree from City University of New York (CUNY), his Masters of Fine Arts from Columbia University, and his doctorate (EdD) at New York

University, this last degree under the mentorship of Gordon M. Pradl. His first college teaching appointment was at LaGuardia Community College in 1980. In 1981, Gilyard became a faculty member at CUNY, Medgar Evers College, where in 1986 he helped to launch the National Black Writers Conference series. He continued at CUNY as a teacher and writing program administrator until 1994, when he took a position as professor of writing and English and director of the writing program at Syracuse University. Since 1999, he has been a professor of English at Penn State University.

Throughout his career, Gilyard has been actively involved in the National Council of Teachers of English (NCTE), including serving on the editorial board and the executive committee and served as NCTE president in 2011-2012 during its centennial. He has also worked significantly with the Conference on College Composition and Communication (CCCC), the world's largest professional organization for researching and teaching composition, for which he served as Chair in 2000. Also notable among Gilyard's professional accomplishments are his receipt of the American Book Award (1992) for his monograph Voices of the Self: A Study of Language Competence, his distinction as Distinguished Professor at Penn State (2005), the Penn State Class of 1933 Medal of Distinction in the humanities (2005), and an Arts and Humanities Medal (2006). In 2005, Gilyard was inducted into the International Literary Hall of Fame for Writers of African Descent.

PREFACE

It is important to say up front this is a very different book. If you are going to get anything out of it, it will be important to understand The Mind Hustler (TMH) metaphor used throughout this work. TMH is invisible negative energy specializing in messing people up by slipping into their minds then rewiring decision-making circuits to broadcast destructive thoughts in the duped person's own voice. The thought attacks will not stop until the person starts hustling backwards (giving up hard fought gains). TMH specializes in running old schemes with the assurance that you will think you are smarter now so you won't get busted later. If that does not work, TMH will agitate old emotional wounds with the goal to get you to co-sign a contract that will lead to your demise. How slick is that? The hustle is over when the victim messes up and falls from grace in front of friends, family, employers and broader society.

You are going to read about TMH from a variety of perspectives in an attempt to expose the most successful trickster of all time. There are brothers and sisters who are being bamboozled, if you will, to go back to harmful people, places, and things left behind in pursuit of a better (hear safer) life. The Mind Hustler can't allow that to happen. TMH fought too hard to mess up lives only to let past victims skip off into the light of a new day. As a mentor, counselor, advocate, and friend to credible messengers around the country it became clear that TMH must be put in deep check before more futures are ruined. Now you know why it was important to put this book in your hands. Let the words of truth, common sense, street smarts, inner awareness, life-wisdom, self-determination and resiliency inform, elevate and protect your mind from you know who.

Quotes appearing above chapters were taken from Elder Wisdom Tweets (alfonsowyatt2) unless otherwise stated.

FIRST EVER INTERVIEW WITH

THE MIND HUSTLER

Special recognition to C.S. Lewis, author of The Screwtape Letters

FIRST EVER INTERVIEW WITH THE MIND HUSTLER

The Mind Hustler has agreed to this interview so readers can be informed and not biased by the material presented in this book. I say read for yourself and see if you are free from The Mind Hustler, battling The Mind Hustler, taking a break from The Mind Hustler, or you are clueless to the existence of The Mind Hustler.

Q. Who are you?
A. I am you.

Q. What do you mean you are me? I don't know you—we never met before.
A. That is how I like you to think of me. You see, my stealth makes it easier for me to do my work. I depend on you not knowing who I am until it is too late. That is why I hate to hear parents tell their children, "Watch out for the boogieman."

Q. Why are you called The Mind Hustler?
A. I will give you the short version. I am skilled at slipping past a person's mental defense sentry, stealing away in the mind, waiting, always waiting for the more opportune time. I have confidence in my hustle to convince the mark that I mean no harm all the while building the forces that will lead to their downfall. At an unguarded moment I strike. Once the person thinks that my thoughts are really their thoughts—they have been hustled. This is why I go to work every day with a smile.

Q. What is the proof of your work?
A. Don't ask me, look around and you will see my artistry, or better yet, think about the times when you heard a sad or even horrific

story and you ask yourself, "I wonder what was on their mind, how could a human being do such a thing?" Now you know the answer. I love taking down the high, low, and in between, rich or poor, known or unknown, gay or straight, incarcerated or free—it does not matter to me. I have to admit, I take special joy when my work messes up a mark and the people who hoped for the best must confront the broken consequences left behind by the hustle. I call it my Two For One Takedown Hustle.

Q. How can you accomplish your mission for so long?

A. That is the easiest question you have asked. I know how to make self-destruction look like fun, of course that depends on what lurks inside the person that I am setting up for the big fall. Look, once a person removes cause and effect from consequence of action there are infinite hustle schemes that can happen. My job is to pick the right one tailored to the person and their circumstance. Good Mind Hustlers must be patient. You can't rush the hustle—you have to take time and set it up. If you bring it on too fast it may not work and if you wait too long the same result may happen. Timing is everything in the hustle business.

Q. Does your success fooling people depend on the person?

A. Yes, people are different, so my approach must be different, yet stay the same. That, in a nutshell is the art of deception. I study my prey. I study their weaknesses but I have to specialize in knowing their strength.

Q. Why study a person's strength?

A. I don't bother too much with weak people who are primed for a fall—they don't need me in order to fail—failure is already lodged on the inside. This person is too weak to address me or stop me—there is no fun in messing up a person who is going to mess up on his or her own. Ah, the strong person is the most challenging and rewarding at the same time. I have to spend extra time figuring out how to turn their strength into a weakness—and then wait for that perfect time I mentioned to go in for the hustle. Sometimes I stand back and admire my work. Most people will never know I did it—they just look at my victim while I am in the wind seeking my next assignment. Sorry I was so long with my response—you can tell I love my work.

Q. You keep talking about being patient; and waiting for the right time, what is this right time you keep bringing up?
A. We turn wrong times into right times—that is an inside Mind Hustler joke. In order to move up TMH ladder you have to be able to recognize instinctively the right moment. To say it another way wait until exposure can create the most damage to the hustled and all the people foolish enough to believe the mark is beyond reproach. Oh, I could tell you stories.

Q. Do you ever feel sorry for the people you hustle? I mean good people have been messed up by you.
A. I cannot feel what I can't feel. You want to judge me by how you feel about me which is precisely why I have to study feelings. If I felt compassion, or love, I can't believe I said love—but it is for teaching purposes, I would never be good at the only thing I know how to do and that is to steal, rob and destroy hopes, dreams and futures. It is easier to take a person down who feel they will

derive a benefit from their dubious action. That is the height of the hustle! Imagine the mark thinks he deserves what he is about to get; if that does not beat all.

Q. *Have you ever tried to hustle a person and it did not work?*
A. Next question.

Q. *Alright, last question, are you nervous that by granting this interview people will learn how you work and not be susceptible to your mind hustling ways?*
A. Nope.

PART I

Essays TMH Does Not Want You To Read

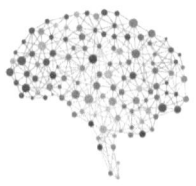

"You are given free will at birth to become anything you want to be in life; it is your responsibility to choose wisely."

FREE YOUR MIND

When I was young, I was fascinated by the mind. I was amazed that thoughts were going on inside a person's head. I remember making up games in an attempt to hear the thoughts of others. As I got older, I began to look at the mind in a new light. I discovered it was not only the center for all conscious and subconscious thought and actions, it also had the responsibility to control life-giving functions of the body. The mind is truly amazing. The mind can imagine. The mind can wonder. The mind can wander. The mind can solve problems. The mind can make problems.

Right now, your mind is trying to accept or reject the very words you are reading. Your mind can push you forward or hold you back. Your mind controls your feelings and feelings control how you see, think and react to things. The mind influences the choices you make or the choices you fail to make. When you start fooling yourself, when you start lying to yourself, when your mind games are so deep that you don't even recognize that you are playing a game, I want you to know that you are in deep trouble.

BEWARE THE MIND HUSTLER: IDENTIFYING SELF-DESTRUCTIVE THOUGHTS AND DISTRACTIONS

Your mind has the ability to create or destroy. Your mind can attack or defend—your mind can extend a blessing or a curse. The mind can be mean or kind. The mind can make wrong seem right. The mind can give strong reasons to try or weak excuses to crash and burn. With that said, The Mind Hustler does not want you to get knowledge that you can turn into wisdom. That is why the mind must be hustled so the truth loses its meaning so that lies can prevail.

The following essays written by me over the course of the last decade, most deal with the mind. Your assignment at the end of each reading is to capture any thoughts you think that will be helpful in repelling attacks from The Mind Hustler. Remember, be honest with yourself—go where you need to go, as deep as you must go, to first identify, then, get rid of "stuff" that no longer define you. One thing TMH hates is honest reflection—so please honestly reflect in the space provided.

FREE YOUR MIND HONEST REFLECTION

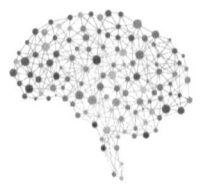

"There can never be lasting external change without the intentional internal death of harmful dysfunctional thought patterns."

FUNCTIONAL DYSFUNCTION

Have you ever purchased one of those "as seen on TV" gadgets? The various products are touted to do amazing things that will make life easier. So perhaps you can anticipate my excitement when the Bright Light Motion Detector was delivered to my door. It was advertised to generate a bright beam of light to identify or deter strangers. When the device was set up, and the light turned on, it was still dark in the area it was to illuminate. The disappointing truth was the device was working yet not working at the same time.

Back in the early 1980's, I thought I wanted to be a family therapist. I took courses at one of the premiere institutes in the country. While the family I engaged thought I was successful in addressing their issues, I left the field feeling there was something else in life for me to do. Before moving on, I got a close up view of how family dysfunction played out in real time. I learned that when you see the "identified patient" in his or her family system, their "odd" behavior made "sense." A person raised in dysfunction can create, largely through magical thinking and strong self-will, a

Functional Dysfunction persona. This person, like the Bright Light Motion Detector, is working, yet not working at the same time.

When you pull back the curtain on many families, it is possible to see a range of dysfunction. Many people learn how to live successfully in spite of their inherited family issues. Moving beyond that blessed cohort, there are some individuals who mask their Functional Dysfunction through overachieving (grandiose thinking), underachieving (victim thinking), or creating a quixotic/quirky personality (over thinking) that serves to hide their real hurt, pain, disappointment, learned helplessness, or low self-esteem acquired while growing up in chaotic families.

Do you know someone who specializes in Functional Dysfunction by habitually taking two steps up and three steps back? Do you know someone who is stuck at a very painful place in their past? Do you know someone always exaggerating his or her achievements in order to paint a lofty picture of self? Now, a different question, are you the aforementioned identified patient (be honest—it could be life changing) enmeshed in Functional Dysfunction?

If so, perhaps you have asked is there a way to end trips leading to a disappointing dead end after dead end? Here are several steps that can shed light on how to fight to live a functional life:

- *You Must Want A Better Life* — What you set your desire on is the first step toward reshaping your life, and by extension, your reality. The next step is developing a short-range, midrange and long-term plan that operationalizes your dream. I caution at this crucial point to watch out for self-created "creative holding patterns" that lull a person into a false sense of progressing when actually there is no significant movement. Here is an example of a creative holding pattern: A person writes a play but will not cast the play but is content because the play is written.

- *You Must Not Quit Because Change Is Slow* — It took years to get where you are—it is going to take time to get where you want to be. Be patient with the change process and with yourself as you learn how to shed dysfunctional behavior, encumbered thinking, and the need to find rational words to justify irrational actions/beliefs about self or others.

- *You Must Seek Expert Help If Needed* — It is possible to want change but never take the steps to change thereby perpetuating, rather than ending Functional Dysfunction. There are life coaches, therapist, psychotherapists and psychiatrists with the skill to help people get free of dysfunctional baggage, debilitating habits and desperate actions tied to their past.

The Bright Light Motion Detector was returned and a full refund was given. There was no reason to keep a light that was not providing light. Likewise, you do not have to hold on to behavior that is working yet not working for you. Please hear there is a present way to address past dysfunction so you can function in the future. Are you ready to shine?

Functional Dysfunction Honest Reflection

"A troubled mind can make enemies friends, or make friends enemies. A troubled mind can bring short-lived comfort, or long-term torment."

TRANSFORMING TROUBLE

I remember facilitating a mentoring workshop at a local community college some years ago. One of the young men in the class spent most of his life living in group homes and juvenile detention facilities offered this gem of earned wisdom when he said, "A counselor once told me just because you are in trouble does not mean you have to cause trouble." This insight provoked him to change his behavior, friends and circumstance. He never dreamed that he would one day go to college and be paid to mentor young people experiencing similar difficulties he successfully faced. This young man became a stellar example of what Transforming Trouble means.

Trouble and life go hand-in-hand. If you live long enough you will encounter some form of trouble from the 'lite' variety to the deep down I don't know if I can take another step type of trouble. Your own doing may cause trouble or it can be trouble visited upon you for no discernible reason. Trouble never makes an appointment; trouble will never wait until you are strong enough to withstand it; trouble does not care if you see it coming or if it must sneak up on you. Trouble will never apologize for causing trouble—trouble is never troubled as long as it is causing trouble to all in its path.

Transforming Trouble is different; yes, it is trouble but it has the power to cancel itself out by opening a door to an opportunity to grow that may have never been seen if not for the initial trouble. This is an important insight if one is to understand Transforming Trouble; so much so, it deserves a deeper dive in the "trouble waters" at the deep end of life's pool. Here are some ways to recognize and be inspired through the process of Transforming Trouble:

- I once worked in a toxic environment in my twenties. I could not sleep for worrying about losing a job I loved. When I finally made the decision to leave, I said these Transforming Trouble words while walking out the door: "If I am ever in charge of people again, I will never create a psychological work environment where people don't know where they stand." This thought followed me throughout my work life, transforming colleagues I was blessed to meet, supervise, and mentor.

- I work with credible messengers—people who were once incarcerated but now work with youth and young adults to deter them from following the wrong path. A consistent factor in the life narrative of most credible messengers I have met, mentored and befriended are Transforming Trouble stories generally centered on honest nighttime self-encounters in their cells. It was at these honest moments that their Transforming Trouble process began.

How does trouble become transforming? There is no single way to answer the question because just as troubles are different; so are one's reactions to trouble. What I can say about Transforming Trouble is there has to be a major mind-shift while one is experiencing trouble. That may not seem logical to a troubled mind. Transforming Trouble does not follow a Linear A to B to C progression. Here is the illusive essence of Transforming Trouble: In order to live trouble free on the outside trouble must die on the inside.

TRANSFORMING TROUBLE HONEST REFLECTION

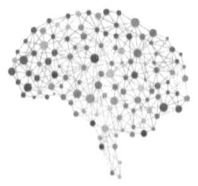

"When you have time to rummage through your mind, be careful to not over refine those thoughts not yet properly defined."

LOST IN RUMINATIONVILLE

Did you know that cows are part of a classification of mammals known as ruminant? Ruminants (i.e. sheep, camels, goats, buffaloes, giraffes) have four stomach compartments where digested food is returned to the animal's mouth a second time as a cud. Cows can stand contently in one place and chew their cud up to eight hours a day. I want to talk about human ruminants—no, they do not chew their food twice, but go through a process of 'chewing' over the same old thoughts, ideas, hurts, or needs.

This leads me to the word rumination that sounds kind and inviting, I must caution there is a dark side. Allow me to offer a clinical definition taken from Wikipedia:

...rumination is defined as, "compulsively focused attention on the symptoms of one's distress, and on its possible causes and consequences, as opposed to its solutions." Nolen-Hoeksema (1998)

Overly pensive people (ruminators) may never believe that they think too much (perhaps up until now), or that their overthinking can cause problems. A person Lost In Ruminationville is doomed to rehash the same issues, problems or brokenness for days, weeks, months—and unfortunately, years, and never come to a solution. The ruminator replays constantly what happened at a crucial point in life, interspersed by an endless 'option parade' of what should have happened. Star "ruminators" are actually able to reproduce somatic symptoms like stomachaches (ulcers), headaches, or general body aches caused by self-created problems.

I would venture to say that many people have spent time in their self-constructed pensive prison. At the risk of creating a new round of thought, let me ask the question why is rumination so prevalent? There are several levels to be considered in response (I am conflating real-time thought with rumination for the sake of illustration):

1. *Rumination as Reverie* — Occurs when thoughts are more fanciful—it is like the mind becomes a phantasmagorical playground where the thinker can have mental fun conjuring up ideas, images and new visions.
2. *Rumination as Problem Solving* — In order for a person to address and properly assess a problem, quality time must be spent thinking because sometimes finding answers takes time.
3. *Rumination as Damnation* — Person feels trapped (tormented?) by thoughts or ideas about others and self. Their thought time is put into chewing "regurgitated" fragments of the past (cud) causing stagnation in the present that negatively influences the future—meanwhile, the core problem is never addressed.

Do you know someone Lost in Ruminationville (#3)? Could you be the person? Don't think about it too long. Beloved, if you are Lost in Ruminationville, I am going to ask you to board a new train of thought (#1) and imagine you have made the decision to take only what you need and leave (#2). As you are riding to Mental Freedom Land, look out the window and you will see a lone cow standing contently in the pasture chewing its cud. Finally, you'll be able to smile because you'll know deep down you are no longer lost in Ruminationville.

Lost In Ruminationville Honest Reflection

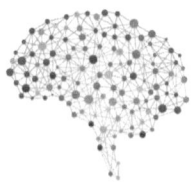

"If you find people to blame for your circumstance you will never be free because the only person who can change your condition is you."

STUCK ON STUCK

Few people will readily admit to being stuck even when it is apparent to others. Stuck is not a good place to be especially in the present heyday of social media offerings like Facebook, Instagram, Twitter and YouTube that thrive on personal elevation through vicarious projection. When a person is stuck, there may be an assumption the cause is due to some form of lack or laziness. Some frustrated helpers may ask, "What's really wrong?" "Why are you stuck?" "Why are you still stuck?" These probes may show either a way out or a way leading deeper into a sticky morass. You may feel better or worse to know that it is possible for people to get unstuck only to become stuck again, on the same, or different "glue trap of life."

So the stuck reflection/inquisition cycle starts anew with self-posed questions like: Is it really me? Is it my circumstance? Do I have bad luck? Am I making bad decisions? Do I have a faulty "stuck" avoidance detector? It is ironic that life coaches, ministers, mentors or wise best friends (the best kind of friend) are able to help people get "unstuck" even when this same advisor may be functioning in a state of stuck, or recently managed to get free. I guess that is what makes a good life coach or counselor; someone who has managed to get free; and teaches the process that led to his or her release.

There are descending and ascending (depends on your perspective) levels of stuck. There is Stuck Lite. Usually a person can work their way out of this sticky holding pattern through time, reflection and moderate effective effort. There is Stuck Medium that may call for a mentor, counselor, life coach or therapist for help. Then there is Stuck on Stuck. This condition may be caused by a heartbreaking relationship, a hope-killing job, or a faith withering thought pattern carried on for years. When one is Stuck on Stuck, it can cause pain and frustration in self and in others. This can lead to bitterness, anger, self-loathing, confusion, or depression. If you find yourself Stuck on Stuck, or know someone you care about in this situation, allow me to offer several hard-earned insights:

- If you try the same things to free yourself and nothing works, you have to try a different strategy. A major aspect of Stuck on Stuck frustration is when a belief over time becomes a self-fulfilling prophecy, namely, nothing you do will work so why bother.

- If you find people to blame for your circumstance you will never get free because the only person who can change your condition is you. It is far easier to blame others, even if they deserve blame, than it is to take personal responsibility for thought, word and deed.

- If you become comfortable in an uncomfortable place in

life, the desire to grow lessens. Helpers need to know about secondary gains. For example, a person figures out why go in debt buying a car when there are plenty of friends and family members willing to offer "free" rides. On the other hand, why get a job when there are plenty of "enablers" who can be manipulated to pay for the latest emergency.

I remember my young and dicey years when I became Stuck on Stuck. My bad decision-making and maddening indecision colluded with my inability to kindle the strength needed to pull myself out of a deep and dark pit I dug for myself. I felt lost and defeated. My desperation drove me to seek God. Talk about switching tactics. It was in this frustrating Stuck on Stuck state that I prayed my first "Soul Be Free" prayer—and it was answered! While I have experienced several Stuck Lite scenarios over the course of my life, I can truly say none has come close to my Stuck on Stuck experience.

STUCK ON STUCK HONEST REFLECTION

"When breaking bread with trusted friends the question is why would you allow fear a seat at the table?"

DEATH TO FEAR

When I was young and easily frightened, I thought it was important to learn how to kill the major movie monsters of my time; namely, Frankenstein, Werewolf, Dracula and the Mummy. I knew Frankenstein was afraid of fire; Wolf Man dreaded wolf bane (or a silver bullet); Dracula hated sunlight (that was better than driving a wooden stake through the heart) and the Mummy, well, I was sure if chased, I could out run that slow moving heap of bandages. I discovered in my childhood years knowing how to kill monsters eased my fear of the same.

Do you have fears that keep you up at night or will not leave you alone during the day? Does your mind bounce between what is to what next? Has your health been compromised by fear? Do you bottle up your fears hoping that will help you cope or practice denial as a method to stave off fear-induced thoughts? We all can suffer bouts of fear; it is what makes us human and in some cases, fear is a response designed to help keep us alive—there are some people, places, or things we should fear.

It is the out-of-control, irrational type of fear that is problematic; a fear of what could be that taints every thought and action by becoming the lens that one's life circumstances are viewed. When the fear machine is fully engaged, it can take a new or old fear and manufacture different imaginary scenarios that somehow become real. The aforementioned fear responses mentioned earlier kick in and real psychosomatic reactions are manifested. This is akin to making up a monster that takes up residence in your head causing a real terror response.

There is a way to vanquish fear just as I was able to do away with self-created or "real" monsters by finding out what can kill your fear. Please know before you can kill fear(s) you must be able to name what it is—it is hard to get past a monster with no name. Some people are reconciled to live with their fears because asking for help is a non-starter. Help could be in the form of talking to a wise friend, speaking to a life-coach, or engaging a counselor, therapist, or psychotherapist (this depends on the depth and duration of fear).

I remember sending a short poem to a brother who was held in a space that was not of his choosing but it became real by his doing. The fear that he lost it all—his standing in the community, family, and friends was real. One day as we reminisced about this dark and fearful time in his life over lunch, I was shocked to see him go in his wallet and take out a small, rumpled piece of paper with these words I wrote to encourage him several decades earlier:

the heart of it
find strength in your weakest moment

PART I: ESSAYS TMH DOES NOT WANT YOU TO READ

let the armor of self be stripped
expose the warrior
no longer wary
of the coming engagement
combatant raise your eyes
strike the telling blow
shout
death
to
fear

Death To Fear Honest Reflection

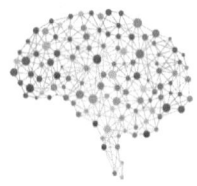

"Mind Games Defined: Player is too invested in the game to quit and too tired to proceed; are you stuck playing games that cannot be won?"

TROUBLED MIND GAMES

I have met and worked with people who live with troubled minds. These sufferers cannot turn off their thought machine. They deal with their forays in and out of reality, fantasy, or paranoid inspired scenarios, all while trying to live a 'normal' life. Thoughts from a churning troubled mind can bring short-term comfort or long-term torment. A troubled mind ponders only negative issues and outcomes.

I don't know why but my mind conjured up a childhood game called Johnnie on the Pony. The aim of the game mirrors what happens to a troubled mind. Let me explain how to play Johnnie on the Pony. A person leans on a wall at arms distance until his (I never saw girls play this game) torso is parallel to the ground. Then players leap on his back one at a time. When the load bearer on the bottom can no longer support the weight of riders on top, he topples to the ground—and then the game starts over with a new person on the bottom.

A troubled mind, like the youngster at the base of Johnnie on the Pony, has too many weighty thoughts piled up. Thoughts from the past collide with thoughts from the present and both fight with the future. This is too much to bear, so the mind may eventually make a command decision to shut down, try to escape, or surrender to mental angst caused by searching for non-existent relief. A troubled mind can tumble like Johnnie on the Pony riders. The ensuing mental game starts and ends with what if, why now, why me, who cares, why bother, what next? These vexing questions create more questions—the definition of troubled mind games. The player is too invested in the game to quit, yet too tired to proceed. What kind of game is this?

What is on your mind? Do you suffer from troubled mind games? Are you processing old recycled thoughts? Are you doing time in thought's dungeon for a "crime" you committed; or do you stay up at night thinking you were falsely accused? I had to learn how to help my mind not fixate on troubled patterns of thinking. It was not easy to acknowledge my personal shortcomings, fears, doubts and compromising half-truths I allowed myself to believe in my failed attempts to find peace of mind.

I had to find a way for my mind to see itself as my best friend and not my self-appointed mental tormentor. The realization dawned on me that as marvelous as the mind is given all of the aforementioned duties and abilities—I was, at the end of the day, the boss of my mind. This revolutionary thinking freed me from me. Please know you can do all of the right things, live a worthy life, pray, meditate, journal, or practice yoga, and your mind can still find ways to play games with you. If this happens, think of Johnnie on the Pony—then say, "I refuse to play the game anymore."

TROUBLED MIND GAMES HONEST REFLECTION

"When the desire to know self overtakes the lack of self-knowledge, this glorious event marks the birth of insight."

THE OTHER YOU IN YOU

I want to talk about the two "yous" in you. This is not a typo. For the sake of clarity, allow me to divide you into You-One and You-Two. You-One is the you that you work hard to project to the public. It is the best you, the endearing you, the inviting you; the what can I do for you you. You-Two is the real you when no one is looking. It can be the devious you, the afraid you, the selfish you, the needy you, the hurt you. In short, You-Two is the you that you do not want people to know is you. The larger the gap between You-One and You-Two, the deeper the subterfuge needed to keep people in the dark as to the real you.

There are people who manage to keep their nefarious You-Two side hidden from friends, co-workers, partners, spouses and the general public in an effort to promote their You-One shining persona. It is never a pleasant experience when You-One and You-Two are revealed as incompatible entities. This discovery, no matter how it is explained, or handled, will shine a light on days, months, or years of artful deception. This can be mind-blowing and heart breaking at the same time.

When doing leadership training, I find it beneficial to use the Johari Window to help people identify a broad spectrum of behaviors while gaining personal insight. Here is the matrix called the Johari Window. According to Wikipedia,

> The Johari Window is a tool to help people understand their relationship with themselves and others created by psychologists Joseph Luft and Harrington Ingham in 1955.... Luft and Ingham called their Johari Window model 'Johari' after combining their first names, Joe and Harrington [Harry].

JOHARI WINDOW

Public I	Private II
Known to Others Not Known to Self III	**Unknown** IV

Window Number One is the *Public Window*, it contains the information you voluntarily make public about yourself to others. Window Number Two is the *Private Window*. It is where secrets live. There are some parts of our lives we choose to make public (moving information from Window II to Window I). However, there are some events, memories, hurts, that are locked away deep in Window II. Even when well-intentioned colleagues, friends, employers, or family members get close to a hidden Window II issue, there can be a shutdown or unexplained attitude shift that is as immediate as it is disconcerting.

People who are volume talkers have large *Public Windows* and a corresponding small *Private Windows*. You can meet this type of person at a party, on the job, or on the street and within minutes, he or she has told you the good, bad and ugly details of their life (TMI). A person with a large *Private Window* can come off as mysterious because it is hard for "outsiders" to find a way in. Window IV (I am intentionally going out of order) is marked *Unknown,* because there are events, words, memories buried deep inside that impact behavior in ways that are unknown to the person. Issues in Window IV are best attended to through psychotherapy. When this type of clinical intervention is successful, information moves up from Window IV into Window II and is spoken aloud in Window Number I (hence the term talking therapy).

Window Number III, *Known to Others Not Known to Self,* is where You-One and You Two co-exist. It is impossible for any person, regardless of motive, guile, or lack thereof, to know how he or she is perceived in real time. Some people may honestly think when cracking jokes about other people that they are funny while the butt of the joke may experience the quipster as an irreverent jerk. A person may think he knows what is best for people and acts without permission, all the while he or she is seen as a controlling tyrant. Window III is where interpersonal conflicts live and thrive in relationships on the job, in houses of worship, in the home, and with friends. The Johari Window is an adaptable tool with deeper complexity that can help individuals illuminate and analyze behavior in self as well as in others.

Are there troubling secrets, past hurts, or slights in your Window II that are suffocating you? Is your incessant need to hear yourself talk or be the center of attention (Window I) constantly getting you in trouble? Are there deep-seated issues that you blocked out roiling in your Window IV? Is there a disconnect between The Other You evidenced in Window III? Like it or not, believe it or not, we are the sum of all four Windows—this is what makes us human, vulnerable, and at times, contradictory. Beloved, remember this behavioral equation inspired by the Johari Window: You-One — You-Two = Only You in You.

The Other You In You Honest Reflection

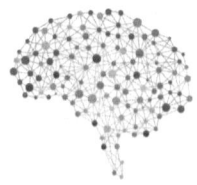

"Know that the mind can travel effortlessly back and forth to the past, present, or future but the body can only exist in the right now."

ANCHORED TO A CLOUD

On a recent flight, my wife was looking out the window and whimsically said to me, "The clouds look so sturdy you could walk on them." We both laughed at the absurdity, yet, the comment made me think. A day or two later, I did some research and found out a cumulus cloud (the puffy fair weather cloud) can weigh as much as 1.1 million pounds given the smaller than a pinhead water droplets dispersed inside. The question I wish to pose is if you were drifting how many of you would place an anchor on a cloud? The answer is not a binary yes, or no—the real answer is it is impossible.

I have not done research on my next statement but I believe I am on solid ground saying all of us may have anchored our thoughts, our pains, our hopes, or our dreams to a cloud at one time or another. You see, reality and fantasy are twins that live side by side. Sometimes it becomes difficult to distinguish one from the other. The fact that the two can become confused may go unnoticed until it is too late. Please know I am not talking about a total break from reality—just a flight of fancy or necessity when one decides to walk on a cloud. Here are some examples:

- If you hide your true feelings behind LOL's, emoji's and trendy sayings when deep down inside you are hurting—you have anchored to a cloud.
- If you are waiting on something, or someone who will never come, yet you refuse to stop looking out the window—you have anchored to a cloud.
- If you find it easier to believe the promises of a liar because the truth is too hard to reconcile—you have anchored to a cloud.
- If you make excuses for someone close to you, or look past your personal weaknesses and always blame other people—you have anchored to a cloud.

You probably get the point by now. Anytime a person treats fantasy like reality it is akin to tethering an anchor to a cloud—it seems real but it is not. This "unreal reality" is amplified when technology is involved. The question must be asked, why waste time trying to make the impossible possible, or think the possible is impossible. That is some straight up cloud talk—dispersed fragments of thoughts. To be honest, there are situations that are too hurtful to bear. Sometimes it is easier to make something up than it is to make up one's mind to deal with reality.

Anchoring one's future on a cloud may not seem like the type of move a concrete thinker would make. It is important to say given a certain set of circumstances, a forlorn sister or brother may opt to hook up with a cloud until reason wins out—or another cloud passes by. No matter what thinking state you are in, be smart and take some advice from the elders when they would admonish, "Make sure your anchor holds and grips the solid rock."

Anchored To A Cloud Honest Reflection

"Make this part of your mantra: I will no longer go on trips that I didn't pack the suitcases for."

CHECK YOUR LIFE-BAGS

In life, it is possible to carry life-bags overstuffed with past hurts, slights, bitterness, hate, bad memories, broken promises, and unrealized dreams. The carrier of this heavy weight can build up strength (tolerance) dragging their life-bags everywhere he or she goes. Once life-bags no longer seem burdensome, the carrier can become comfortable with this uncomfortable situation. I want to put heavy life-bags one may be carrying, dragging, or have in storage, on the scales of life and ask this question—is the price of guarding, toting, or worrying about life-bags worth all the pain and suffering? If you are looking at your life-bags in the same way, or perhaps in a different light, hang on, not to the handle mind you, but to the following life-bag insights that can be transforming.

LIFE-BAG # 1

The contents of this life-bag were packed, as all life-bags are, at birth. It contains the sum total of the owner's interpretation of his or her lived experience. The negative contents have a way of simultaneously shaping and misshaping how you deal with reality, as well as how others see you. Old hurts can cause new pains when you look in your life-bag and you grow angry or confused. This constant action and reaction can render the thought of unpacking pointless.

LIFE-BAG # 2

The contents of this life-bag are in total disarray, prompting the question, "Who packed this bag?" The sad answer is that the owner has allowed people to drop their personal disparaging opinions, thoughts, or indictments inside the bag. This extra weight is designed to minimize, and hurt; thereby giving the "dumper" a false sense of "lighter" superiority over the one duped into carrying unwanted biased weight.

LIFE-BAG # 3

The contents of this life-bag are unrecognizable when the owner peeks inside. This "mystery bag" can lead the carrier to experience deep psychological issues that only a trained life-bag professional knows how to unpack and help to reorganize.

It is time to Check Your Life-Bag. It is time to empty out old bits and pieces that are no longer you. Some of the items don't fit because you have grown emotionally and spiritually. Get rid of "stuff" you no longer wish to wear, or is a mischaracterization of who you really are, or blatant lies intended to belittle and malign you.

I remember when I was forced to check my life-bag in my twenties. I had created a complicated, multilevel thought apparatus designed to protect me from probes from others that may or may not have meant me harm. In retrospect, this compartment of my life-bag became too hard to maintain. I had to discover the "room-making" truth: Less can surely be more—as in more peace, more love, and more joy.

CHECK YOUR LIFE-BAG HONEST REFLECTION

"I fought thoughts of fear, doubt, anger and discovered I was the boss of my mind. This revolutionary mind-find freed me from me."

THE ENEMY WITHIN

There is a war going on seemingly with no end in sight. Every day, soldiers are drafted or volunteer to continue the fight. This conflict causes real and collateral damage to individuals, families, friends, co-workers, communities and nations. The battlefield is littered with angry, dazed, wounded, or dead soldiers—some fought valiantly, others reluctantly, yet, these warriors vow to keep fighting because that is all they know. Beloved, I am talking about the inner fight that pits self against self.

Anyone, given the right—or perhaps wrong set of circumstances, can battle self. If you ever asked why did I react in a particular way that had harmful personal consequences—or wondered for days, weeks or years, how did I wind up in this forsaken place? You should know that there was a fight, it was you vs. you, and one of you lost. How could this be? Perhaps a look at several micro-case studies will shed some light.

- *Combatant # One* was fired from three jobs over the last 18 months. He feels unfairly picked on by "the powers that be" so much so that he always feels he must fight to protect his position. There is a feeling of justification when he stands up for his rights especially when he senses the charges levied against him are trumped up (which is all the time). What is not known is that after breaking free of his demanding (he would say abusive) parents he vowed never to allow another person to rule over him again. He is proud that he sticks to his guns no matter the consequence.

- *Combatant # Two* has great difficulty trusting people. Her learned epiphany is that people lie, cheat, and betray. She experienced a tragic hurt many years ago. Anytime a person tries to get close, she creates a situation where there is a fight and ends the relationship—even if she cares about the person. She notices that her emotional range is not what she wants but she finds it is necessary not to be too warm with people or let down her guard because this can allow an opening that can cause pain on top of her pain. Her demand to everyone she meets at some point or other is to say, halt who goes there.

This is what inner war looks like and the learned response is attack, attack, attack, before you are attacked. Any thoughts of living in peace, evaluating confrontations on a case-by-case basis seem like a foolish luxury at best. The combatant has become skilled at spotting dangerous foes near and far. It is imperative to neutralize or vanquish all identified opponents. This war, fought in the mind, fueled by passion, mixed with animosity, is ignited by fear. After each fight, there is a need to assign blame to the person(s) responsible.

So now, the stage is set for a final showdown calling for the execution of The Enemy Within. All of the usual suspects have gathered. The question on the mind of the assembled voyeurs in the gallery is who will step up and pull the trigger? Is it you mom? Is it you dad? Is it you abuser? Is it you supervisor? Is it you spouse? Is it you sibling? Is it you lover? Is it you God? There is a gasp when it all becomes clear—not from the witnesses gathered to watch. The gasp, more like a moan, comes from the victim. The identity of The Enemy Within is finally revealed; it has become painfully clear that it was you warring against you all of this time.

THE ENEMY WITHIN HONEST REFLECTION

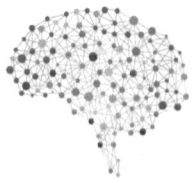

"Light can create shadows; the same light can eradicate shadows—this contradiction must be reconciled in order to grow and thrive."

FAMILY HURT

Sometimes a smile can tell a deeper story—case in point. As I was leaving an event where I was asked to bring the invocation for a local congressperson, I wanted to catch the eye of the security guard as I walked to the exit. She allowed me to walk in without waiting behind the people on line when I entered the building. I thought it would be only proper to say thank you for this courtesy on the way out. Little did I know that behind her winning smile were years of hurt visible in her eyes.

I went over to her and asked a few questions. She began to talk about the hurt her family has inflicted upon her. She searched for the words as if to find a balance between truth telling and not speaking badly of her family. She said that no matter how hard she tries her family finds ways to make her feel like nothing because she has a dream for herself. People who have grown up in loving families may have compassion for the young woman but may miss the deep pain caused by those who should have loved her, should have wanted the best for her—namely her family.

There are people of all races, belief systems, age, sexual orientation, political persuasion and zip codes who have experienced Family Hurt, a topic not high on the conversation list because of lasting stigma and shame. Sometimes it is hard to know what issues are behind the smiles of people who have been wounded, limited, denigrated, plotted on, ridiculed, unsupported, or ignored by family.

If you have experienced Family Hurt, or you know someone who has, here are some suggestions that may offer options to suffering in silence, dangerously acting out—or, at the very least, let you know you are not alone.

- Don't allow yourself to isolate — yes it is normal to want personal "down time" but when down time becomes no time for others or for yourself that is not always helpful and seldom healthy.
- Engage in activities that make you feel good like reading, going to plays, volunteering, singing, cooking, traveling, journaling, working out, running, walking, Zumba dancing, listening to music — praying etc.
- Turn off the mental videotape machine that constantly replays the time, place, and person who visited Family Hurt on you; and please don't talk to people whose only gift is to reinforce what is on the tape never offering viable solutions.
- Know that you will pay a deeper emotional price for hating the family member who caused you to suffer than they will ever pay as objects of your hurt and anger.

- It is possible to create family not related by blood but joined by love.

While I could not change the lived experience of the young security officer with the beautiful smile, I looked beyond her smile and peered deep into her soul and told her,

"Don't allow, "hope chokers," even if it is family, stop you from going after your dreams. They made a choice to discourage you because you want to be somebody in life and likewise you must make a choice to be who you want to be in life."

As I walked toward the exit, I paused, walked back to the security desk and handed the young woman my card and said to her, "I am now your Uncle Fonzo; I will not hurt you; all I will ever do is encourage you, make you laugh, and pray for you." When you think about it that is what families are supposed to do.

Family Hurt Honest Reflection

"The dualistic power of hope can kindle a deep desire to persevere in the face of overwhelming obstacles while inspiring others to do the same."

PHOENIX RISING

The Phoenix is a mythical bird that was able to rise up victorious out of the ashes of destruction. In my role as mentor, role model, and public theologian, I can unequivocally say that I have met sisters and brothers who capture the true spirit of Phoenix Rising. I want to pen this open letter to you (you know who you are) and to any others who had to rise up (or are fighting to rise) from the fire of hellacious familial, personal, social, psychological, legal, financial, or spiritual circumstances. When I hear your story, especially childhood atrocities committed against you and siblings, I wonder if I could have withstood the same constant pressure, heartache—and yes, anger that no child should have to bear. No one picked his or her family. Life is a random process that over time turns into one's destiny. It is not fair to have to drink from a bitter cup that you did not pour. Because I am hardwired to give advice, I hope you do not mind a few spirit jogging bullet points I pray can help you:

- I tell people who have gone through the fire that at some point in life it is important to find the power to destroy what tried to destroy you like negative thinking, recurring harmful memories or self-doubt/self-loathing.

- Learn from the past but don't live in the past. It is clear but should be stated that the past cannot be altered. What was done was done and cannot be undone; no matter how hard or long you try or cry.

- One of the gifts of life is the ability to change for the better. Change can be painful in the short run but ultimately rewarding. Change, in the form of moving on from a crushing circumstance, may be minimized by folk who have never been trapped in pain's vice grip. The caring, uncaring, or the fatigued may offer sayings like: Build a bridge and get over it; be like The Beatles and Let It Be; When the going gets tough the tough get going. This all sounds so easy on paper but oh so difficult to put into practice—but you must find your way even if the way you seek is hard to identify.

- Remember to take care of yourself. Do things just for you—this is not being selfish. If you give and give and give without refueling, you will find yourself eventually running on empty. You cannot help others if you cannot help yourself. Put you on your to do list. Refresh yourself. Spoil yourself as you love yourself—ashes and all.

- Find time and space to enrich yourself spiritually. Keep blaming of self and others to an absolute minimum. Blame will not put out the fire that occurred in your life. When the smoke clears up enough for you to find the key that opens the door marked forgiveness, find wisdom and the strength to walk through.

The Phoenix in literature was part of the genre known as mythology. The Phoenix I am writing this missive to are, husbands, wives, children, sisters, brothers and friends. You may have descended deep down into the fiery abyss of mental illness, physical or sexual abuse, depression, betrayal, loneliness, family dysfunction, grief, abject poverty, incarceration, or debilitating illness, but guess what, you are still here! Your strength is a testament to the resiliency of the human spirit. See your true self as Phoenix Rising victoriously from the ashes of life.

PHOENIX RISING HONEST REFLECTION

PART II

PERSONAL STORIES OF RESILIENCE, RESISTANCE AND RESURRECTION

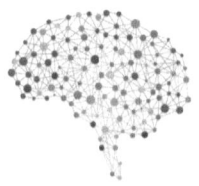

"A little bit of light can expose what is hidden in darkness; that is why you should never extinguish your light."

THE MIND HUSTLER EXPOSED

The Mind Hustler studies the mark's strengths as well as weaknesses with a particular focus on tendencies—especially when a person experiences stress, anger or confusion. The more data TMH has on you the better it is to tailor a slick custom-made takedown plan. TMH firmly believes that anyone can be hustled given the right time and circumstances. As stated, TMH likes a challenge so there is special joy going after people who believe they are beyond the hustle because of past battles, internal resolve to keep it moving—or ego.

I have a calling to help people who have made mistakes in life. I know there are some folk out there who may have a hard time with my calling. I would imagine this person never messed up; never committed an act that he or she wishes never happened. I can say when I was a puppet of TMH that I made some mistakes that put my future in jeopardy. It is the memory of these times that keep me focused on the feasibility of making a new start in life.

As I was conceiving the flow for this book, I knew it was important to have the voices of people who have had or are having encounters with The Mind Hustler. I gave to prospective writers a template to write an essay, a letter to TMH, or any other expression that would capture how TMH is able to create mayhem. Here are authentic witnesses' personal accounts that may help you peep TMH before a trap is set for you. While I provided a basic outline and minor edits where needed for the sake of uniformity and flow, I accepted the writer's interpretation of the assignment.

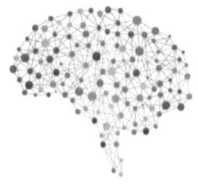

"Hustling Backwards Defined: Taking two steps up and three steps back yet never thinking you owe a step just to get back to where you started."

THE MIND HUSTLER
~B. CINCERE WILSON

I most certainly have been hustled by The Mind Hustler. I was convinced that street life was for me and the only way I should live. I saw the glitter, gold and glamour of crime, and I wanted in more than anything else. I quit college to sell crack because The Mind Hustler had me thinking school was a sucker's play. I thought I could make a lot of money working for myself instead of paying to have someone teach me how to work for somebody else—and then came the violence.

I grew up in the Patterson Projects in the South Bronx where violence was nothing new, but in the 1980s, we saw an escalation of violence that was unparalleled to anything seen before. However, we also adapted to the life-style of violence and drugs to the point where it became normal. Only The Mind Hustler could make us think that way of living was normal. I went against everything my parents taught me and ended up in prison with a sentence of TWENTY-FIVE YEARS TO LIFE.

While doing my bid, I had many experiences with The Mind Hustler. When I wanted to straighten my life out because I no longer wanted to live the way I was living, The Mind Hustler convinced me to wait until tomorrow to get started. Tomorrow became the next day until it was next year or when I got out of the box (solitary confinement). I wound up in the box because The Mind Hustler convinced me I had to do something to maintain my status although I wanted to change the way I was living. That is what hustling backward looks like.

It was in the box where I realized that The Mind Hustler is a part of me. For me, this foul mofo is self-doubt; procrastination, insecurity, and thinking my problems were other people's fault. At least, that's what I used to believe. Once I recognized that I was holding myself back, I taught myself to see The Mind Hustler in all the forms he came at me even though I did not know what to call it at that time. The more I made moves to help myself, the less I saw of The Mind Hustler. In fact, I almost got caught believing I had defeated him. This sucker is crafty and patient. He never dies.

The way I deal with The Mind Hustler is to stay true to who I am, because life will test me and The Mind Hustler is always watching. The Mind Hustler is a liar; I can no longer afford to believe the lies because I am an Incredible Messenger and there are more lives at stake than my own.

> *Ben Cincere Wilson is a program assistant for the Institute for Transformative Mentoring, where he leads trainings, offers college and career counseling, and coordinates program operations. He once served as a high school equivalency in-*

structor at Exodus Transitional Community Inc. For over 15 years, he has facilitated GED, mentoring, poetry, and theater programs in correctional facilities. Additionally, he designed a creative writing course with the primary focus on college prep. As a mentor, Cincere has helped young people navigate the pitfalls of the street life that leads to prison by helping them focus on formal and informal educational pursuits. While helping these young men and women, he won an "Honorable Mention" award for his submission to the prestigious PEN Prison Writing contest (2015). Cincere obtained a Bachelor's Degree from Bard College.

"If you want something of value out of life that you don't presently have, you must be willing to put in valuable time in order to get it."

MESSAGE TO TMH: FEAR WON'T STOP ME
~KHADIJAH ALLEN

I am a product of two addicts both addicted to crack/cocaine. For those of you who don't know DRUGS are the leading cause of death, separation, dysfunction, and dissolution of families, especially in the African-American community. Thankfully, there came a point in my mother's life where she decided to make a change by going into rehab. Of course, this was a wonderful thing because it meant no more staying with granny and being disappointed because I stayed up late waiting for mom to come home during the time of her addiction.

I worked hard in school. My parents stressed how important it was so I dived right in! I was in the Honors Program from first grade. I entered every spelling bee and oratory contest presented to me to impress my parents and make them see that I required more attention than for whatever reason they were neglecting me. In the sixth grade, I was awarded Orator of the City and was sent to compete statewide. I reminded my parents for weeks about the contest because in my mind if they could see how "good" I was doing in school they would pay more attention to me.

I won the oratory contest but lost the fight for my parents' attention. I was devastated. From that day on, I realized my relationship with disappointment was something that I could not face. My worst fear is to look forward to or work towards something that might not or does not happen. My fear of disappointment crippled my life. At 16 years old, I told myself that I am not going to finish high school so I dropped out. I wouldn't apply for certain jobs in fear that I might not get them. I am an excellent poet, hairdresser, actress, mentor, etc. but because I had already told myself I would not be successful at any of those things, I would do them temporarily then drop them by the wayside. I always knew I was talented and smart but The Mind Hustler had me living in fear that I would be disappointed if things didn't happen the way I planned.

When I was about 20 years old, I began to have this reoccurring dream. In the dream, I'm sitting on a bench and every person I've ever met in my life is stopping to visit me on the bench, sharing their plans, dreams and goals with me, and then they would get up and go about their business. For some odd reason I could not move from that spot. I had that dream about four times before I realized that it was a metaphor for my life. Everybody I knew was moving on with their lives and making things happen and I was refusing to give my dreams and goals a fair shot because of my fear of being disappointed. That dream did two things for me. It depressed me AND it woke me up. If everybody else could push forward and try new things then so could I!

Within two years, I had obtained my GED and driver's license, enrolled in college and got a new job. I was so proud of myself, not because of what I had accomplished but for the courage to try

PART II : PERSONAL STORIES OF RESILIENCE, RESISTANCE AND RESURRECTION

these major life changes. Ten years later and my dislike for disappointment is still very much present but it no longer stifles me; not because things always work out as planned but because even when they don't I keep in mind that I have to KEEP TRYING. That consistent drive has helped me get five promotions within the last 10 years, move into my own space, start my own business and participate in the most beautiful and fulfilling personal and professional relationships imaginable.

> *Khadijah Allen, born and raised in Brownsville, Brooklyn, NY attended I.S. 41, Harry Van Arsdale High School and the College Of New Rochelle. At the tender age of 19, Khadijah began working for Housing & Services as an Anger Management Counselor and Front Desk Clerk. She worked there for seven years before she was offered the position as School Aide with the New York City Department of Education in 2008. Working in a Transfer High School, She engaged young people and families so well that she was promoted to Parent Coordinator and part-time Advocate Counselor. Additionally, she also worked part- time with Jewish Child Care Association as lead mentor for The Arches Transformative Mentoring Program from 2012-2016. Since then, Khadijah has transitioned into the role of School Secretary and started her own business, Operation Heal 100 Hearts, a trauma centered support network with a goal to encourage healing through strength, self-assessment and resiliency. Khadijah is now a resident of Bedford-Stuyve-*

sant in Brooklyn working diligently to service her Brownsville community within her role as Secretary and Conflict Resolution Specialist at Brooklyn Democracy Academy High School. In this capacity, she mentors her peers, runs support groups and leads by example with positivity, consequential thinking, compassion and love.

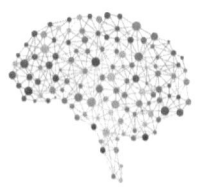

"If you don't build your own dreams, someone will hire you to build theirs." (Offered by the author)

LETTER TO THE MIND HUSTLER
~JASON ACOSTA

Dear Mind Hustler,

As I sit back and reflect on the many times I have encountered life challenges and the pressures put upon me throughout my childhood, I realize that only I have the strength and ability to make positive choices. Mind Hustler, you come in many different forms and expose yourself at some of the most difficult times. It is almost as if you are the little bad guy on my shoulder encouraging me to make the wrong decision. I see you in the media, in society, in my community, and beyond.

Growing up, I felt pressure to follow and engage in behavior that led to consequences, despite knowing it wasn't the right decision at times. It only felt right because it was what I saw happening around me. I felt I had to abide by the unspoken rules of the neighborhood where I lived. With experiences in foster care, the criminal justice system, and educational inequities, I learned that you reappear throughout life and can evolve if I allow you to do so.

Mind Hustler, I have news for you; you can no longer influence me. I have the ability to create my own future and write my own biography. Mind Hustler, despite encouraging me to follow the wrong crowd leading me to negative consequences in life, I have persevered. I need you to understand that I have dreams; that throughout my life I faced hardships that now fuel me to be the best I can be. I learned how to conquer your game Mind Hustler. I learned that there is much more to life than what I saw and experienced growing up. I learned that I am in full control of my life. There is nothing you can do to stop me from reaching my dreams. I understand that you need to get over The Mind Hustler in order to build your dreams because if you do not, someone (The Mind Hustler if allowed) will hire you to build theirs.

> *Jason Acosta is a proud native of the South Bronx and a product of New York's public schools. Jason currently serves as a Program Manager for the Office of Teacher Recruitment and Quality at the NYC Department of Education where he oversees several long-term pipeline programs as well as teacher recruitment for physical education teachers across NYC. Jason works closely with two Mayoral Initiatives including: PE Works and NYC Men Teach, a program centered on the recruitment of male educators of color. In addition to his work at the NYC DOE, Jason is a former founding board member, and former Chair of the Academic Subcommittee, for the Cardinal McCloskey Community Charter School, where one-third of the student population is comprised of children living in foster care. Jason*

also serves on the Board of Directors for the College Access Consortium of New York (CACNY), comprised of 300+ organizations working together to remove barriers to college access for NYC students. Most recently, Jason joined the DreamYard Young Professionals Committee, an organization in the Bronx that is mission driven by arts and social justice. In his spare time, Jason mentors at Eagle Academy for Young Men in the Bronx, as well as Project Morry, a nonprofit organization that empowers young people to establish a positive future. Lastly, Jason holds both a Bachelor of Science in Social Work from Marist College and a Masters of Social Work from Fordham University where he specialized in leadership. Jason had an opportunity to share his expertise in his role as adjunct professor at Long Island University where he taught a course titled, The Lives of Adolescents.

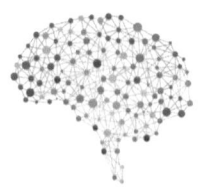

"The only thing that can defeat hope happens when one loses faith in hope."

THE MIND HUSTLER
~MARGARITA MONTGOMERY

My description of The Mind Hustler is that it is thorough in getting to you, holding on to you, and killing you if it can. TMH can start the hustle when you are a hurt child with low/no self-esteem. With that ammunition, it will take away your total existence from the world and especially from yourself. The hustle is cunning, you hear the whisper of your pain and will do negative things to yourself to relieve the pain, be it drugs, alcohol, sex, etc. If you realize that you've been hustled, you better fight for your LIFE... no, fight for your very SOUL or DIE!

My discovery of The Mind Hustler working in someone I attempted to help is the same discovery that others found when they tried to save my life. The person was successful for at least 10 years, then one day she allowed TMH to whisper in her ear. It wasn't overnight but eventually she believed the lies saying, "You can still hang out." She knew she was being lied to but thought she could make them truths. My friend began the worst journey of her life, I say the worst journey because the first journey she went on she didn't have a son, or material things.

I was guiding my friend on her positive journey, showing her how it worked for me and giving her suggestions that I received. Although she did it her way, she did put together 10 years. Then it happened. I would call her and she would be too busy. My knowledge of the life let me know she was back into people, places, and things that she did not need to be involved. The voicemail messages were not returned and when they were, I got this, "its ok," from her. Then she stopped all communications for about five years. My friend allowed TMH to push all the struggles that she endured to the back of her mind. She lost everything she had—her health (she almost died), her job, apartment and her precious son.

"The dualistic power of hope can kindle a deep desire to persevere in the face of adversity while inspiring others to do the same."

Letter To The Mind Hustler
Margarita Montgomery

8/12/59 and counting

Mind Hustler
666 Depths of Hell Place
Hell, 66666

Psst, Mind Hustler,

You thought you were going to kill me by having me destroy myself with your guidance didn't you? You are a low being starting on me as a 7-year-old and having me suffer trials for so many years. Well, read this and weep! You thought drugs and the terrible deeds done to me were going to be the death of me but even in the midst of pain, heartache, no self-worth, and feeling that no one loved me I wanted a high school diploma and got one. I wanted to do something monumental, so I went into the Army and got an Honorable Discharge in spite of being an addict the whole time.

I still remember the talk I had in high school with my teacher about his friend Jesus and although it was almost 20 years before I called upon his friend. Guess what, He answered and showed me that He was all the love I needed. His written Word told me that he would never leave nor forsake me, most of all He couldn't, not wouldn't, but couldn't lie. Jesus put some people in my life that you tried to kill and some that never experienced you because all they ever knew was Him. He let me see that I was someone, I was His child and that He loved me no matter what.

Marjorie Montgomery

P.S. Check the date I'm still here.

> *Margarita Montgomery (Margie M.) was raised in Jamaica, New York by a foster family that included two sisters and one brother. She is a high school graduate and received an Honorable Discharge from the United States Army (Specialist 4th Class, Personnel Management & Medical Supply). She later retired as a correction officer. Margie is the mother of two adult children and "Mima" to three grandsons. She is an avid church member and is loved by a host of folks, most of all by her husband she calls her hero.*
>
> *In doing the assignment, I went back as far as I could remember (4 years old) and cried. There was not a lot of happiness in my life back then. There was so much sorrow, pain, loneliness and so little if any love. I cried because that little girl doesn't hurt much anymore. She still has scares; and she still has scars. She knows her big girl self has fought to keep her alive by helping her find inner peace so now they both can survive. Thank you for this task. It was a gauge to remind me how far I have come. Thank you for the cleansing.*

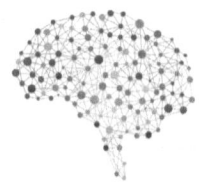

"Some people have self-sentenced themselves to do voluntary solitary confinement in the dungeon of sad yesterday."

THE MIND HUSTLER
~JAMEL MASSEY

SPOKEN WORD

Hear Ye, Hear Ye
May I have your attention please...
Hear Ye, Hear Ye
The Mind Hustler is seeking to deceive;

Those focused, faith-rooted, and on track...
The goal is to confuse, seduce, and distract;

Thinking the grass is greener on the other side...
Another soul has fallen to the power of the dark side;

Convinced to put their views and values on the shelf...
Performing the greatest con of all, hustling self;

Living in the shadows of their very own strengths...
Removed from the circle of the "talented 10th;"

Once upon a time on the path to success...
But by heeding the wrong voice, their life now a hot mess;

From being full of potential and community involved...
To becoming a statistic of the same problem they tried to solve;

Facing these challenges while striving to stay clear...
Seeking guidance and support while laying their souls bare;

Seeking keys to the doors leading out of hot spots...
Not knowing the Mind Hustler keeps changing all the locks;

These struggles and temptations change offenders into healers...
This is the journey and plight of those we call
Credible Messengers.

Jamel Massey currently serves as a Program Director for Exodus Transitional Community, and is a training and support facilitator with Community Connections for Youth (CC-FY). He received his mentorship, facilitation, and circle practice training from the Credible Messenger Institute – which is sponsored by The Credible Messenger Justice Center; and The Institute for Transformative Mentoring located at The New School – Center for New York City Affairs. As a trained Credible Messen-

PART II : PERSONAL STORIES OF RESILIENCE, RESISTANCE AND RESURRECTION

ger armed with personal experience, a background in human services, and a message of hope, he encourages others to take full advantage of the spiritual and social resources available to help them improve themselves and the overall quality of life within their neighborhoods. With his message, he inspires others to continue along the path of personal change, community empowerment, and societal redemption.

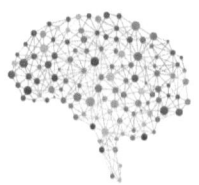

"Please do not be tricked, no matter who you are or where you come from, you must always remember—there is no future in the past."

THE TRICKSTER
~WILLIAM ERIC WATERS

It starts at a young age—the voices in your head. The negative messages you hear from others, even your parents, from society, and more recently from social media. They are usually negative, insidious, and seemingly enduring. They make their way into your mind and embed themselves, attaching to the brainstem. Just the other day, I was talking with a 12-year-old white female who is part of a youth group in a church in Bronxville in Westchester, New York. The youth group was visiting a mentoring program within the church. The program mostly works with men and women who have been imprisoned, many of them for decades from when they were young.

The young girl and I talked about the self-fulfilling prophecy embodied by mostly negative voices that insinuate themselves into people's minds, telling them that they are nothing, that they will amount to nothing. When they are referred to by a positive adjective, it is turned on its head, like *super*...predator. Young people are more susceptible to the voices of these prophets of their personal doom who oftentimes negatively label a young person and thus direct their lives into a downward spiral, and the depths of detention centers, jails, and prisons.

The girl talked about those negative voices that even appear in her well-off community. Even at this young age, she is aware of her privilege and the protection she will be afforded from those voices more so than a 12-year-old from Brownsville. During the course of our conversation, I mentioned the poverty of Brownsville in Brooklyn, New York, and the wealth of Bronxville, and how resources, or the lack thereof, will determine the story of their lives and where they end, or end up. It begins, or ends, with that story, what young people are told about themselves, what they can or cannot be, or what they can or cannot do.

Various cultures incorporate a Trickster into their story telling. In Norse mythology it is Loki; in African-America folklore it is the Signifying Monkey. The Trickster referred to throughout this work is external to the culture and the people it targets. Of course, there is a different Trickster in Bronxville than the one in Brownsville. This is why, in part, many of the men in the mentoring program, from neighborhoods like Brownsville, have spent almost more than three times in prison than this girl has been alive in Bronxville.

They had heard those voices predicting their doom when they were young. They are now much older, but they know the voices are still present and that they must be vigilant and battle against them, sometimes daily, or risk ending up back in prison. Many of them work through organizations and in their communities to disrupt what has been called the prison pipeline flooding the prison system with young Black and Brown boys and girls from

PART II : PERSONAL STORIES OF RESILIENCE, RESISTANCE AND RESURRECTION

neighborhoods like Brownsville. Many of these men and women are now credible messengers. There is a message in this work that is being done by credible messengers. They are the foil to the Trickster, and recent evidence validates that their work with our young people is not only valuable and impactful, but also has already begun to stop the flow of the prison pipeline.

> *William Eric Waters, AKA Easy Waters, is an award-winning poet, playwright and essayist. He is the author of three books of poetry and one novel, including Black Shadows and Through the White Looking Glass: Remembrance of Things Past and Present (co-winner of the 1998 Edwin Mellen Poetry Prize). Waters is a Credible Messenger, having grown up in the Mary Housing Projects in Brooklyn, NY. He has over 25 years-experience in criminal law. For the past 20 years he has worked for two social service organizations, the Osborne Association and currently the Fedcap Group, where he works on two mentoring projects for 16-24 year olds. He also manages a mentoring program for men at Sing Sing Prison. Waters has earned awards for his criminal justice work, including the Ralph Bunche Bridge Builder Award, which was renamed the William Eric Waters Bridge Builder Award, and the Esther House Prison Ministry Award. Waters has a Master's Degree from New York Theological Seminary and Bachelor's Degrees from Albany University and the College at New Paltz.*

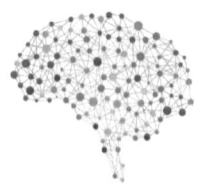

"Once you find your mission in life, take what was designed to destroy you and you destroy it."

LETTERS THAT HEAL
~JESSICA A. MALDONADO

Dear TRAUMA,

I see you don't discriminate… I've been up all night trying to find the right words to say to you… It was really nice to reconnect with you! You became my best friend over the last 37 years. I have learned so much from you over the years, so much so, it became my lifestyle. You have played a very important role in my life decisions. I blamed you for getting in the way of me building and maintaining healthy relationships, for getting in the way of my blessings by saturating me in fear and anxiety. You blocked every love vessel in my body to a point I didn't know how to love myself and I was afraid to love others.

When I buried my son (who was the love of my life) at 18 years of age, I buried my hopes and dreams. Paralyzed in hopelessness, I saw not one good bright day before me. It took me some time and it was very painful, but I faced you, now I'm embarrassing you. I am now nurturing my inner child who grew up afraid and anxious. I've been keeping her safe and saturating her in lots of love. You helped shape me into the person I am today and that is a powerful and fearless humanitarian, and for that, I truly appreciate you.

However, I've learned that nothing lasts forever, so with that said, I no longer embody you. You no longer hold a fear space in my heart. I will no longer allow you to dictate my future and block my blessings. I found my heart and there is no room in here for you. Before I conclude let me tell you a little more about who you shaped me to become. This might sound funny because you cause so much pain and uncertainty in people's lives, but I would like to thank you for all the pain you caused me. It prepared me and now I lead a purposeful and meaningful life.

I challenged myself to further my education after having checked out of school in middle school. I am now pursuing my Master's Degree in Mental Health Counseling with an interest in Thanatology—the study of death and dying and the bereavement process. I am now a proud mother of my daughter Jalia Jones Maldonado who I call my rainbow child and a proud daughter to my Queen, my mama, Joanne Sawyer.

My troubled childhood led me to become the first and currently the only violence intervention specialist at Kings County Hospital for Kings Against Violence Initiative (KAVI) where I lead and carry out all interventions. In addition to my career path, I've turned the horrifying time of my life to greatness. The death of my son led me to become an advocate for New York City Administration for Children Services Safe Sleep Initiative. I volunteer at the Kings County maternity department facilitating safe sleep workshops before moms are discharged. My newest project is working on is developing my own birth, postpartum, and bereavement doula business.

There is power in letter writing...

Your time with me has expired, so PEACE!

Love and Light,
Jessica A. Maldonado

> *Jessica A. Maldonado serves as a credible messenger and trauma intervention specialist at the Kings County Hospital Emergency Department for Kings Against Violence Initiative (KAVI), where she provides therapeutic bedside response and bereavement support to patients and families impacted by interpersonal violence. She is a powerful, passionate advocate who knows firsthand how the loss of a child and the grieving process puts a strain on the family and community. Jessica's willingness to share her story and her strong sense of support has helped parents, families, and communities heal after a trauma or after losing a loved one. She is active in her community offering presentations at local schools dealing with trauma and resiliency, mobilizing crisis response teams, holding space for healing circles and providing bereavement support in communities and hospitals.*
>
> *Aside from Jessica's career as an intervention specialist, she serves as a birth, postpartum and bereavement doula. Her passion and commitment to her city is helping families restore hope and overcome the stigma often associated with mental*

health, death, and dying. Previously, Jessica worked at a funeral home where she witnessed the trauma people go through after losing a loved one. Her dream one day is to shift the paradigm of how people process trauma (loss) and heal in healthy ways. Jessica holds a Bachelor's Degree in psychology, and she is pursuing a Master's Degree in mental health counseling with a focus on thanatology (the study of death, dying and bereavement process). She is a proud mother of a 17-year-old daughter Jalia Maldonado whom she calls her rainbow child.s

"Running from the truth is a race that will never be won no matter how fast you make yourself run."

A LETTER TO MY YOUNG PEOPLE
~PERRIAN S. GLASBY, CREDIBLE MESSENGER

I was once swindled and sold an ounce filled with something I thought I wanted. The Mind Hustler who sold me this ounce was able to convince me that it was the best on the block. That ounce was a lifestyle of making poor decisions. To my young readers you are faced with making decisions every day. My biggest fear for most of you is whether you can differentiate right from wrong. Please always keep in mind that one ten second decision can cost you a lifetime.

Many of us have met The Mind Hustler and have purchased some of his product. Whether it was an ounce of peer pressure, or an ounce of greed, we must educate ourselves in order to be able to ward off the Mind Hustler's attempt to sell us something that is detrimental to our lives. I call out to the readers and credible messengers who will gain insight from my warning and use this letter as a tool to encourage the young people who come after you to be aware of The Mind Hustler.

I provide an alternative to The Mind Hustler's products. We must become leaders rather than followers; we must value ourselves as well as others. This mindset won't happen overnight, but I implore you to take the necessary steps to remove yourself from The Mind Hustler's long list of customers.

> *Perrian S. Glasby began work as a credible messenger at the age of 20. He started working for Children's Village as a mentor for The Way Arches transformative mentoring program under the Young Men's Initiative, and the NYC Department of Probation. During Perry's five-year tenure at Children's Village, he worked in juvenile justice, residential, preventive care, and foster care. In 2017, at the age of 25, Perry graduated with a Bachelor's Degree in Criminal Justice from Monroe College, a month after graduating from the Institute for Transformative Mentoring (ITM) housed at The New School for Social Research. Perry is currently employed by the City of New York Administration for Children Services working in the Department of Youth and Family Justice Close to Home program as a Placement and Permanency Specialist. Perry is also enrolled full time at John Jay School of Criminal Justice seeking a Masters in Public Administration specializing in management and operations.*

"Don't think just because you want to do right that your mind will automatically agree to help you get right."

LETTER TO THE MIND HUSTLER
~EBONY WOLCOTT

Dear Mind Hustler,

You told me that once I came home I would be free; that the streets would praise me and I would take the place of all the others who sought to be down. Funny thing is, all you did was sell me a dream. I wasn't the block's hottest and I certainly was not free. You said I would come out stronger then I went in, but in all actuality, incarceration made me vulnerable and I became weak. My whole life was now public record, no privacy even in my private moments. I can't eat and don't want to sleep because for all I know someone is still watching me. There was a greater sense of freedom behind the bars in a cell.

Everyone I meet has control over my freedom; none of them want to see me "free." Those people gave me restrictions, not for my safety, or the safety of the community, but for me to slip. They wanted me to miss probation, or to not go to school, or be suspended so that I would be remanded. I wasn't smarter than you were so I made mistakes over and over again—mistakes that set me back, stole some years and gave me time. That was time to think, time to regroup and get ahead of the next curve hopefully. I now had to use the system to my advantage because it only wanted to consume me.

> Ebony is an artist, mentor, and youth advocate from Brooklyn. She is an alum of the Institute of Transformative Mentoring at The New School for Social Research. Ebony has facilitated Artistic Noise workshops with youth impacted by the justice system across all five boroughs of New York City, including the annual S.W.A.G. program at the Department of Probation. In addition to her work directly with youth of Artistic Noise, she has presented at workshops in Washington, D.C. at The Crittenton Foundation's In Solidarity We Rise seminar, and The Healing Justice Summit at Columbia School of Social Work organized by How Our Lives Link Altogether (H.O.L.L.A.). Ebony has spoken on panels at New York University, John Jay, and Hunter. Her time at Artistic Noise has provided a safe space to enhance her skills as an artist, and develop non-profit management skills. She hopes to use everything she has learned and continue spreading awareness about life after lockup to the people who don't understand, or may need guidance, or mentorship. She is currently working with Artistic Noise Co-Founder Francine Sherman and Boston College on a project called "I Am Why" which is centered on the lived experiences of young women who have emerged from juvenile justice and other correlated systems.

"In order to see, you first must look; know this, just because you look does not automatically mean you will see."

A LETTER TO THE MIND HUSTLER
~BISHOP DR. DARREN A. FERGUSON

Dear Mind Hustler,

Your words and outward actions say "I Love You," but behind the scenes, your behavior says otherwise. When your requests are fulfilled and your asks are granted, you are the best child, parent, family member, coworker, church member and community partner ever. It seems that the word 'no' does something to you. When you don't get your way, your responses are of tantrum-like proportions. Your demeanor, your speech, your texts, emails and your responses in worship are all affected.

Many have been mind-hustled into acquiescing to your whims simply to keep the peace because your passive-aggressive meltdowns are epic. No public displays of anger; you have never had an outburst that is observable, but you have found clandestine tactics – calls, texts, social media posts – that rage against all that defy your desires. Your absence – physical, emotional, and spiritual is glaring when you are in protest.

I write this letter to say that I see you, hear you and pray for you. I understand that experience has dictated that you don't react well to disappointment or rejection. I realize that your default setting is to engage in mind-hustling tactics to achieve your goal. I know that you are attempting to protect your heart, but you have encased a broken heart that desperately needs healing. Please know that safe heart-space exists, but it can only be found when you release yourself from the cocoon of mind hustling as a protective tactic. I will continue to love you anyhow and there is nothing you can do about it.

Love and Blessings

> *Darren A. Ferguson serves as Pastor of Bethel Baptist Church in Orange, New Jersey. A reformed Mind Hustler, he uses his life experience as a father, husband, community leader, author, singer/songwriter, wanna be comedian, returned citizen and lover of humanity to be God's utensil. He lives in Teaneck, New Jersey with his wife Kim, his daughter Naia, and doggy-daughter Sarah (aka RahRah).*

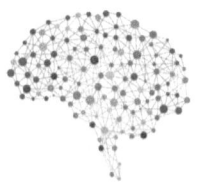

"Fight hard not to allow your personal smallness to get in the way of your spiritual greatness."

BEWARE THE MIND HUSTLER
~TYISHA JACKSON

(Inspired by the Institute For Transformative Mentoring)

The first job I landed when I came home from prison was one of the worst experiences of my life. It was in an armory in Niagara Falls N.Y. I was given a mop, a bucket, and told to clean a huge gym. I immediately felt degraded as if this job was punishment for being black and formerly incarcerated. Once back home, I graduated from a six-week building trades program for women that served as a back door for women to get into the union. After being kicked out my first go round, I had every intention of being at the top of the class.

I worked in construction for nine years. It felt like it was the only field that paid a decent amount of money for a returning citizen although you were told you would not have long to live after retirement because of the pollution you breathe in and the amount of wear and tear construction takes on one's body—especially a woman. My bills were catching up to me. I was desperate for work.

I went back in the work program for public assistance and they sent me to a car dealership that hired on the spot. You had to be a criminal to do a good job, good at lying to people of color and taking them for whatever they had just to get a commission or be underpaid every week. I felt horrible hurting my people. The Mind Hustler made me think that this was all I was worth. The last thing I wanted to be was a house nigger.

My mom had suddenly died and I decided to go into the medical field. After graduating from a 15 month Medical Assistant Program with honors, I was rejected from job after job because of my record. I finally landed a position in that field. I did not know how to act. I was grinding so hard (I felt like I had something to prove) that I really didn't consider employees around me who worked just as hard to get in their positions. The Mind Hustler made me feel I deserved more than anyone else did so I worked harder. I wanted to be the helper, front person, back office manager, secretary, and medical assistant. Nobody cared because I didn't care about anybody but my hurt self.

> *Tyisha Jackson brings knowledge, dedication and a passion for connection as she works to support and advocate for individuals and families facing challenges. She has worked as a Parent Coach with Good Shepherd Services (GSS) Family Court-based Parent Support Program since 2014, and was promoted to Program Coordinator in 2017. As a Parent Coach, she empowers caregivers to understand and be heard in Brooklyn Family Court processes and designs activities that*

promote youth and family unity and bonding. Tyisha works to support parents using a holistic approach to reduce barriers that parents experience physically, emotionally, and socially. Ms. Jackson uses her personal and professional experience to cultivate loving credible positive relationships; she creates family everywhere she goes. As a Parent Coach, Ms. Jackson has sat on several professional panels advocating for trauma-informed care in the engagement of caregivers. In addition to her work with GSS, Tyisha has started Incredible Credible Messengers, a 501(c)(3) organization that supports individuals returning to their family and community after incarceration through trauma-informed practices. Ms. Jackson is proudly at the forefront of New York City's Credible Messenger movement and consistently demonstrates the power of authentic caring relationships to change lives.

"People going through life troubles must know it is important to name their inner adversary because you can never defeat what you cannot name."

BEWARE THE MIND HUSTLER
~KEONN SHEPPARD

SPOKEN WORD

We all want to be accepted, accept that with no exceptions
So we design our personalities, we get hurt and make corrections
We divide ourselves by our differences
and ration out our affections
We break down acquaintances by race, gender and class;
so that each has their own sections
As if morals, ethics, philosophies are based on our complexions?
Or my checkbook, brain, or gender type is our only connection?
We close our tight-knit clique, so that those that don't fit or
kept out for our protection,
So, if you don't seem to be exactly like me within
you are a bad selection!
So now, a traitor, with a face like yours,

gets through with no detection
You handpicked or your constituent and still lost the election?
Had your deacon grab the offering,
he bounced with the collection
You got screwed, wearing a condom and still
die from the infection
But I know that love is not a shade and that evil can vary
I know any relationship is a risk and that every risk is scary
And so I Journey to find 'Open Arms'
while listening to Steve Perry
Praying folks don't think that 'Real Love' is 'Ironic',
if Alanis sings with Mary
But most times is to the contrary, 'cuz most folks act contrary
And they'll sooner steal your 50 cents then let you ride the ferry
Hacking holes through wholesome hearts with the hatchet
I'm trying to bury
So, these days when Jimmy is in a Jamm
he can't even count on Terry
And they fuel the fire for your beef and then they let you stew
Your enemies buy your CDs and spend their free time playing you
But you hurt me, you must know me, so the folks that do are few
We act like animals, live in cages in our whole world zoo!
Life is no longer a game; we play Monopoly with no clue
Mind Hustler screams, "Go to hell," and then, because of him, I do
We throw garbage on our roses and complain about the view
But if you nail both God's hands to the Cross then

who's going to carry you?!?
My suggestion is you marvel in the way you've been designed
Know the vantage point is Most High
when it's you and He combined
Just go one day at a time, live in love and you'll be fine
And you will free yourself, by locking up the hustler in your mind.

> *Keyonn Sheppard is an Artist/Activist. His career spans 30 years, beginning as a founding member of the Citykids Repertory Company. As a vocalist/emcee, he has toured the world opening for artists from Pharell Williams and Erykah Badu to DMX and Wu - Tang Clan. He is currently a credible messenger mentor facilitating the Institute for Transformative Mentoring's Youth Development/Anti-Recidivism Program at The New School for Social Research. He also serves as Assistant Pastor of New Beginnings Tabernacle of Deliverance in Brownsville, NY.*

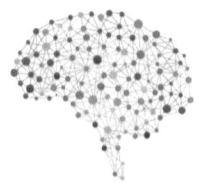

"A very important life lesson is never see personal weakness or setbacks as a reason to throw in the towel oppose to an opportunity to grow."

THE MIND HUSTLER AT WORK
~JOHN DUCKSWORTH

Unlike sports, there is "no time out in life" especially for those who have experienced the ills of the streets or the anger of the courtroom, or correctional institution. When someone is fortunate to get beyond that period in his or her life, the game is not over. I use the word game only for lack of a better word but it is not a game, not by a long shot. There is always that voice some call "stinking thinking" and others call "criminal thinking." However, tonight I will call it The Mind Hustler.

Far too many times persons who have climbed from the bottom and are well on their way to the top forget what it was like going down to the bottom. As well as what it's like to be on the bottom. We forget! We listen to The Mind Hustler and hear that voice that says, "you are smarter, slicker." We hear that voice that says we've got it to together so nothing can stop me now. We start out cutting corners, telling little lies, showing up late. Before you know it, we don't show up at all.

One of the side effects of being down and finding our way upward is that for some we embrace the idea that the world owes us something; therefore, we want to get paid. We want our ship to come in. It's amazing how many persons I have met over the years who have earned a GED and claim that they will never work for less that 40K a year or get an Associate's Degree and say, nothing less than 65K a year. Sure, they worked their way far from where they were but this is not the big payday. As one speaker has said, "Paper brings paper."

But that Mind Hustler starts to whisper into your ear, "You played by the rules and now it's your turn to get paid." If we continue to do the work, we will get paid. The key is continuing to do the work. Doing the work also requires that we protect ourselves from The Mind Hustler. Some of the ways in which we do that is by being selective with whom we spend our time. Another guard against The Mind Hustler is how we spend our money and how we decide to recreate and with whom. And, God forbid, if we are still under the watchful eye of community supervision don't forget that Big Brother is watching. Along the way, there will be those who disappoint, repress, put down, refuse to help, and even some who will hold you back. You cannot give in, give up, or give out. Let there be no doubt in your mind, The Mind Hustler does not take time out, neither can you.

John, born in Harlem, USA attended New York City Public schools. He acquired an Associate Degree from Dutchess County Community College, a Bachelor's Degree in Liberal Arts from the State University of New York, a Master's Degree in

Professional Studies from New York Theological Seminary with a concentration in counseling and a Master's Degree in Public Administration from John Jay College of Criminal Justice with a concentration in management and organization. In 1985, John went to work for The Salvation Army in East Harlem, NY. After four years, he elected to become a Salvation Army Officer and was admitted to the School for Officer Training. In 1990, he graduated, was ordained, and commissioned to the rank of Lieutenant and later promoted to the rank of Captain. He served as an Officer in Philadelphia, PA., Brooklyn, NY, Essex County, NJ and Boston, MA. After 17 years with the Salvation Army, he resigned his ordination and commission. Subsequently, he has provided leadership to court based programs, community corrections, probation and juvenile justice agencies, private correction corporations and social service agencies in New York, New Jersey, Pennsylvania and Washington, D.C. His various roles have expanded from experiential to providing direct service to middle and senior management and government agency executive teams. He has been the recipient of numerous awards and has been published. He is married to Joan and they have two daughters ages twelve and eight years old.

"A person's outer glow is in proportion to their inner glow. The more a person glows on the inside, the brighter the glow on the outside."

FIRE
~GREINY RODRIQUEZ

(The author of this essay is not a credible messenger but she has a credible message.)

One of the most horrifying moments in my life was realizing I might not have a roof over my head and dinner on the table. Over two decades ago, my mother invested most of her savings in a small beauty parlor shop on the upper West Side of Manhattan in New York City. My mother's bank account was soon thriving and we were living the "good life" as we saw it. One day it was all gone and we were living paycheck to paycheck and struggling to realize if we would ever reach that point in our lives again.

What a cold winter it was in 2010. Heaters kept us warm because coats did nothing but add extra weight on our shoulders. Keeping the beauty parlor warm and convenient for customers was a struggle so a portable heater did the trick. Getting to school and meeting my mom in the beauty parlor was a brisk painful walk in the cold. My thoughts kept me warm. Walking up the steepest hill in New York City on 181st Street, I had time to picture myself on the best vacation my family and I had planned for that summer fantasizing of the warm radiant Dominican Republic sun flashing on my face as I floated over the clear blue ocean. These thoughts roamed my brain every day as I walked up that hill barely breathing the thin air and having my eyes water constantly due to the cold.

Yet this walk from school was a little different. As I approached the beauty parlor, I noticed everyone was outside without his or her coats or extra layers. Within the crowd, my mother caught my attention. She was sobbing so hard I almost felt her pain just by looking at her. She was staring directly at the beauty parlor burning to pieces barely acknowledging my arrival. Over 20 years of what she had built was disintegrating right in front of her and it was out of her control. I ran to my mother asking what happened. I was anxious and did not know how to deal with the situation. Frankly, my mother did not know how to deal with it on her own. She just hugged me and cried and we cried together.

The firefighters arrived shortly after I did and told us to step away from the premises. "What will we do now," my mom kept asking? "My children eat because of this place. My children have a roof over their heads because of this place. Without this, we will not survive. What am I going to do?" she kept repeating as she sobbed some more? This was when I really started to worry. My mother had always kept her fears and concerns to herself because she never wanted to worry her children. This day however, she could not keep everything bottled. From across the street we stood and watched as the firefighters seemed to notice there was not much to salvage from the parlor. As they approached my mom asking her questions about insurance and things I was too young to understand as she wiped her tears away and answered. She put on the "strong woman" face she always shows to others—no sign of weakness after the tears were wiped away.

"What a Mind Hustler," I say to myself. The vacation fantasies were long lost in my thoughts and were just dreams. The cold began to feel crisp and the air thinner. How could I have possibly helped my mom out of this one? I was too young to work, too proud to turn to my father who probably wouldn't have helped anyway, and too resilient to stay with my arms crossed and not do anything. Every day after that I decided to give my mom some words of encouragement and remind her how much I loved her. Since I could not help financially, I thought to myself that at least I could help emotionally. I would remind her that even though she had a rough day she still came home to children that loved her and a cozy bed I made up when she came home. I am not sure if it actually helped, but seeing a smile on her face was enough for me.

Moments like these I learn to be grateful for everything I currently have and everyone I have in my life. After that day, I tend to tell myself, "It could always be worse," and it can! My mother could have died in that fire, God forbid, or have been seriously injured, but she wasn't. Everyone that was in the beauty parlor was able to evacuate safely without any injuries. I learned that life is much more valuable than we think. Just some optimism can change the mood of a horrible situation. With this said, The Mind Hustler did not bring my family and me down, we grew closer together. We are grateful for each other and for what we have because, it could always be worse.

> My name is Greiny Rodriguez and I am everything but average. I am a Dominican woman in search of a remarkable future with a goal to impact others and leave my mark so that I will be remembered. Helping others is my passion and I plan to do so by becoming a physician assistant. I come from a single parent household, born and raised in The Bronx. I decided to pursue higher education in Geneseo State College, New York. I love upstate New York and I love proving others wrong. When I walk into a classroom of this predominantly white institution, my peers seem unaware of the fire that burns within me until I begin to speak. The fire that motivates me; the fire that makes me extraordinary; that fire is what makes me everything but average. My name is Greiny Rodriguez and this is not the last time you will hear about me.

"A person with larceny in their heart is hard to help because they view the intentions of people through the lens of a hustler, thus mischaracterizing some people who genuinely want to help."

BEWARE THE MIND HUSTLER
~SEKOU SHAKUR

Over the past year, I have had to give thought to this concept of The Mind Hustler. I recently started a new job as a reentry case manager and have been entrusted with new responsibilities, developing new relationships and having to become mindful of old practices. My job calls for me to provide Metrocards to clients who are in need of transportation to and from work, appointments, workshops and more. It has crossed my mind a time or two how easy it would be to forge someone's name or request their signature for some document that needed signing only to use it to steal Metrocards or gift cards. I clearly know that this thinking is criminal and must be challenged, yet the thought has come up.

The second challenge has been working in a female dominated work environment while maintaining my sense of decency. It has become so easy to get involved in office romances today. I see it often and hear the stories from my colleagues even more so. Maybe it has always been this way and we as returning citizens are just now facing it. Coming home from prison after 34 years and being confronted with a willing and at times aggressive female coworker can be challenging. Understanding myself, and being mindful of "The Mind Hustler," I have been able to overcome and hold on to the values I have set for myself and the professional approach I bring to my job; and the trust that people have put in me.

This third and last reminder has been the hardest at times. There are days when clients who are demanding, insensitive, aggressive and even verbally abusive, confront me. I have been threatened and called out by clients; and would have, without a second thought, responded with the same energy if not more. I must remember at all times that I represent a class of people who are not given many opportunities to come to the workplace without critique and a watchful eye. I am better than my fears and shortcomings. Also, just as important are the challenges that the men I serve come with and the need for me to provide service to them. This is a better example of conduct under duress.

I hope the examples mentioned above how The Mind Hustler jumps out and challenges us from time to time will come to mind. If I were to offer any advice it is surround yourself with people you can talk to and confide in; people who will keep you grounded, humble and honest.

Sekou Shakur is currently employed at Urban Youth Alliance's Jails to Jobs (J2J) Program as a case manager with over 30 years of experience working within the intricacies of people management. He works in Manhattan and The Bronx serving clients who are 22 years and older who have had negative experiences with the criminal justice system. His work in the criminal justice field allows him to assist members of the community with housing, employment, substance abuse and mental health concerns. He provides education and vocation opportunities, as well as Cognitive Behavioral Therapy by way of support groups and one-on-one mentoring. Sekou spends his free time as a public speaker and activist around issues such as limiting solitary confinement in New York City and state jails and prisons to no more than 15 days. Developing strong relationships are at the foundation of everything he does both professionally and personally.

Sekou is also working with the Correctional Association of New York to put an end to long term solitary confinement, both in State and city prisons and jails through the non-profit organization, Returning Aging People from Prison (RAP). He organize, campaign, educate and lobby the community and elective officials around the need to release the elderly, infirm and dying men and women who have served their respective sentences and are denied parole because of the nature of their crimes. He is the co-owner of KEST Construction, a small company that offers training and employment to formally incarcerated men to give them a sense of dignity and self-worth through employment. KEST has secured employment for over 200 men and women since 2014.

Brother Shakur is executive director of A Challenge to Change (C2C), a non-profit addressing criminal thinking and *behavior in prisons/jails settings, educational institutions, work places and the broader community believing in the adage, "As a man thinketh so he remains." Sekou Shakur is a witness to the power of change and the transformation of the redemptive soul and the tenderness of a helping hand. Returning to society after 34 years of incarceration in 2014, he has made it his life mission to share his story, lend his experience, and offer his time with as many as possible.*

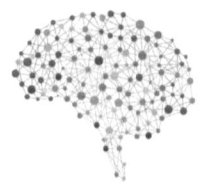

"Who is the real you inside of you? If you don't know, or perhaps forgotten, go inside yourself and look for the real you so you can let go of the manufactured broken image created by the old you."

MY SEARCH FOR SELF
~TODDRICK BROCKINGTON

I f you ever talked yourself out of doing something that is the best thing for you, know you have met The Mind Hustler. Just think of the definition of hustle. It requires energy—energy that is caught up in the negative vortex of The Mind Hustler's—energy that is toxic and inspires shame. It is characteristic of The Mind Hustler to not only perpetually plant seeds of self-defeat and self-sabotage but to get the targets of deception to think nothing of themselves.

For me that gap was understanding the value of change. I invested a huge portion of my life in crime and punishment. The return on that investment was serving almost 33 years of my life in youth and adult correctional facilities. It took almost 16 years into a 25 years to life sentence for me to consider changing. Then it took a few more years of "self-inventory" to peep the game and recognize that I had been hustled. Shortly after, I came to a startling discovery when I realized through self-reflection, self-honesty and an objective evaluative assessment, that I had been the culprit the entire time. I set out to first, educate myself on myself because I lost myself. I hated myself, so I hurt myself, my kind, and humankind.

Secondly, I began to educate myself formally, or should I say, take education seriously. Along this eye-opening, up-lifting journey, I found myself. I now had something to say when I would have nothing to say—my value system shifted—I let go of the hustler/hustled mentality. I had to come to the realization that in order to stop being hustled, I had to stop betting on the negative; stop being a pessimist. I began to value others and myself. I have come a long way. That is not to say that sometimes I get thoughts from The Mind Hustler trying to take me back to a dark place. Now—I breathe, because I believe I can achieve.

> *Toddrick Brockington, from Brooklyn NY, earned a GED, Associates Degree, and Bachelor's Degree in Behavioral Science. He now lives on The Lower East Side of Manhattan. He is a working actor, director, and writer. He has appeared in, "Escape At Dannemora," "Orange Is The New Black," "Power," and "Law And Order."*

"God save me from my friends; I can handle my enemies." (Unknown)

FRIENEMIES
~G.S. BROOKS

Frienemies are friends that do or say things that you would expect from enemies. What makes this type of relationship dangerous is these are people with whom you are familiar and have developed close emotional bonds over months or years. They may be childhood friends and people whom you believe you know and trust. Therefore, it becomes very difficult to sever emotional ties. Many people will do things for or with frienemies that they would not normally do for people they are not emotionally connected to. After I was released from prison in 2004 after serving a 6 years sentence I was sentenced to 4 1/2 to 9 years for "directing a sale." I ended up doing 6 years because of my gang affiliation. After that I made up my mind to live a legitimate lifestyle. For me this meant staying away from hustling that landed me in prison in the first place.

My plan was very simple; find a job, save money and invest in my own business. I had no previous work experience or a GED, but what I did possess was the determination to make it, and a Building Maintenance Certificate from Gowanda Correctional Facility. I was excited to be home, and even more excited to reunite with my childhood friend who had done over a decade in prison himself. I loved him like a brother. My love for him superseded any love I had for a woman and even some family members. You see, we grew up together, we hustled together, and we struggled together. We had fights together, where we were back-to-back "shaking out" with grown men. We got arrested together selling drugs out-of-town. This was my brother, my right hand man—my comrade. When I finally saw him, it was magical. We hugged and laughed for several minutes as if we had just gotten away with robbing a bank. I think that in the back of our minds we never thought we would see each other again.

We were both on parole, but despite that fact, we decided to have a drink in celebration of reuniting. So there we were talking loud, drinking, telling war stories, and in a state of perpetual euphoria. I eventually told him that I was out of the game for good. I told him I had discovered that I was talented in writing and fashion design while in prison. I planned to use my skills to land a job in the industry or start my own business. He was impressed by how much I had grown intellectually and was amazed by my fashion sketches I shared with him. I told him that we could be partners just like we were in the streets. The only thing that would change is the product. Instead of selling coke, dope, crack, or weed we would be selling books and clothing, and possibly get a movie deal.

He agreed, but he had plans of his own. He was already hustling and now I gave him a reason to hustle harder. He felt we needed money to fund my talents. I told him that we should both get jobs and save, but he was against that. He said that he had never worked before and wasn't "working for no white man." I understood that logic, after all, once upon a time I felt the same way. I figured that eventually he'd come around IF I led by example. A few months later he was having problems because he owed his "connect" money and he needed "work" to keep his "block flowing." He kept asking me about my old connects. He wanted me to introduce him and he promised that both of us would "eat." I did not want to introduce him because, although he was a loyal friend, he had bad money management skills. When we were young, he would spend "work" money on having a good time when he got caught in the moment. I cannot count how many times we were in a club and he would have "re-up" money on him and spend it on bottles, weed, girls, cabs, or hotel rooms. Since he kept asking, I felt for him and despite my reservations, I made the introduction. I vouched for him with one of my old connects who also was a very good friend of mine. I made it a point to tell my connect that I would not be involved and that I was out of the business. I told my childhood friend that I did not want anything out of it but make sure that he took care of the connect because he was a close friend of mine as well and I had love for him.

 Everything was going well I assumed but a few months down the line my homeboy owed my connect a few thousand dollars and was looking for another connect to make it up. How did I find out? I had missed several calls from my connect; when we finally spoke he told me that he couldn't find my homeboy. He wanted me to contact him so we could meet. He reiterated that he had only given my homeboy some "work" on "the strength" of me. Here was my dilemma, neither my connect nor my homeboy were slouches, meaning that they both were comfortable using extreme violence to get their point across. My connect though had a lot of money and "goons" he could easily put money on my homeboy's head. I did not want a war between them, I had love for them both, but my homeboy was wrong. Whose side should I choose? If there is a war, should I get involved? Would I have some type of responsibility if someone was severely injured or killed? I was placed in a compromising position even though I had no vested interest in their business at all.

What can we learn from this?

Being a credible messenger, you must be willing to sever ties with anyone connected to an illegitimate lifestyle because you can be pulled into it even if you are not directly involved or benefitting from it. You can be with someone who did something to someone else, or is a target because he/she is making money or affiliations, and you can get caught in the crossfire. You can be with someone who is being investigated by the police and just by hanging out with the person you can get your picture taken and become part of someone else's indictment and end up serving time for a crime you had no knowledge of.

Part of your duties as a credible messenger is to live responsibly, not only in your work but in your personal life as well. Your life decisions can cause ripple effects that can serve to pulverize the entire movement. The moral responsibility that we have to ourselves, the people we serve, and the formerly incarcerated population are consequential. One bad decision can ruin economic opportunities for millions of returning citizens and assistance to their families. Equally important are the lives that credible messengers affect. The mentees will not have that voice of empathy, reason and direction to turn to, which will leave our communities in the chaos that we are devoted to redirecting. As a credible messenger, you have to make the decision to do the right thing even when nobody is looking.

I got my homeboy and my connect together and settled the matter. My connect decided to leave it alone on the strength of me. My homeboy did not think it was a big deal. He is not an enemy, and did not intentionally put my life in danger, but the decisions that he made could have had a devastating effect on my life. As it concerns personal responsibility, my decision to connect him was inexcusable no matter my reasons for doing it. That was a bad judgment call on my part, but equally erroneous was my attachment to someone I had outgrown. I put myself in danger by maintaining a relationship with someone that I knew was living an illegitimate lifestyle. I've learned that I have to develop relationships and associate with people that are either crime free or are on a similar life's journey.

> *G.S. Brooks is the author of The Psychology of Freedom a nonfiction book that describes the antisocial pathologies that the prison experience creates. He is a student of life, after being raised in juvenile facilities and prison, G.S. Brooks began to write while in segregated confinement as a hobby and a doorway out of the criminal component of his life. When he finally returned to the streets, he launched his own company and became an advocate for the at-risk community. G.S. Brooks*

has established himself as a writer, speaker, publisher, graphic designer, video editor and community leader. He has worked with several re-entry organizations and mentored at-risk defendants in his work with public defender attorneys. He has spoken at various juvenile facilities across the nation to encourage youth offenders to be productive members of society. He is on the board of Extreme Change, a non-profit 501(c)3 organization in Phoenix, Arizona. G.S. has worked with College Initiative to encourage the formerly incarcerated to seek higher education. He speaks on various panels to advocate for the at-risk population. He volunteers for non-profit organizations and uses his personal finances to help youth in need reshape their lives. He is currently working with prisoners to encourage them to invest in their inherent talents and do something constructive with their time. G.S. Brooks is a graduate of the Credible Messenger Institute (CMI).

PART III

Fortify Your Mind In Your Own Words

"Some people confuse having a desire to change with actually changing. If there is no executed plan of action then desire becomes its own reward."

SEVEN STEPS TO DEFEAT THE MIND HUSTLER

Without vigilance and consistent effort, the following steps are just words on a page. In order to counteract TMH it is important to link will to power. Will is the desire for change; power is the muscle to get it done. Too many people fail to link will to power. This is like being in a car stuck in neutral. It has the power to move but no movement will happen until the car is in gear. Bring will and power together and create willpower to help you overcome obstacles. Now that you are at the end of the book, fill out what you are willing to stop doing and start doing in order to defeat The Mind Hustler.

1. *Connect...* To positive influences and spirits that speak to where you wish to be in life. It is difficult to stay positive surrounded by negativity. Remember, if you want something new, you have to do something new. Don't let TMH fool you into thinking that changeless change is change. So many people can't connect because they come right up to the door of change and refuse

to knock. It is equally disappointing to see a misconnection because a brother or sister went through the door only to leave because change is not easy. You have a spirit light that exposes inner truths hidden in the dark. If you connect to your spirit, it will connect you to your destiny.

IN ORDER TO CONNECT I AM WILLING TO:

STOP DOING:

START DOING:

2. *Select...* Good friends that will tell you the truth and not just what you want to hear. Some friends cannot speak the truth because there is no truth on the inside. It is important to judge who is a real friend and who is a fake friend. In case you need help, a fake friend has perfected the ability to appear like a real friend (sounds like TMH to me) when all the while he or she is bringing you down. Responsible adults admonish young people to choose their friends wisely; the same can be said to adults.

IN ORDER TO SELECT, I AM WILLING TO:

STOP DOING:

START DOING:

3. *Respect...* It is important to respect every step of the journey that got you where you are right now—hopefully in the state in which you were born, and that is free. Respect the people who stayed with you; the people who prayed with and for you, helping you along the way. Respect yourself and your accomplishments. The moment you take rebuilding your life for granted is the opportune moment The Mind Hustler is trained to look for and to pounce.

IN ORDER TO RESPECT, I AM WILLING TO:

STOP DOING:

START DOING:

4. *Disconnect...* You must make a decision to disassociate from destructive people, places, and things. You can learn how to juggle a live grenade yet one failure will undo your past success (you can't play with some things). It is hard to disconnect

from something that seems pleasurable that is why The Mind Hustler makes self-destruction look like fun. Believe me, no one can afford to laugh at a life that is wasted.

IN ORDER TO DISCONNECT, I AM WILLING TO:

STOP DOING:

START DOING:

5. *Perfect...* Perfecting yourself is not the same as trying to be perfect, just being the best version of you. Can you say you have found the best you in you? Vow to grow mentally, socially, spiritually as you master life lessons. Also, commit never to hustle backwards because there is no future in the past.

IN ORDER TO PERFECT, I AM WILLING TO:

STOP DOING:

START DOING:

PART III : FORTIFY YOUR MIND IN YOUR OWN WORDS

6. *Collect...* All that is out there for you that is beneficial to where you want to go in life. Collect your hopes, Collect your dreams, Collect a winning attitude. Remember what you value generally is what you protect. Value your sacrifices; value your time; value your journey, value your freedom—and value your future.

IN ORDER TO COLLECT, I AM WILLING TO:

STOP DOING:

START DOING:

7. *Protect...* You must fight hard to protect the gains you have made—never take the work of personal transformation for granted; and never grow weary in the never-ending battle that pits self against self. The Mind Hustler does not want you to believe that it is a war you can lose. Stop fighting you and fight that which comes to steal, rob, and destroy.

IN ORDER TO PROTECT, I AM WILLING TO:

STOP DOING:

START DOING:

"When the desire to know self overtakes ignorance of self know this glorious moment marks the birth of insight."

FORTIFY YOUR MIND IN YOUR OWN WORDS: GO BACK TO THE FUTURE

Find a quiet space where you will not be disturbed for say an hour. You are going to go back in time and find your younger self. You now have the opportunity to mentor the young boy or girl you found. Write down the advice that the older you would give to the younger you.

_____
_____
_____
_____
_____
_____
_____
_____

"If your life is headed in the wrong direction, don't ignore your inner voice whispering...You Turn."

LIFE TURNING POINT

What was the turning point in life when you were sure you would not go back to your old lifestyle? How did you know this was a real turning point—or did you know? Do you recall a turning point that did not hold up, if so, why not? Write your thoughts below.

_____

_____

_____

_____

_____

_____

_____

_____

BEWARE THE MIND HUSTLER: IDENTIFYING SELF-DESTRUCTIVE THOUGHTS AND DISTRACTIONS

"There are truths residing deep in the heart waiting for the day of liberation."

PERSONAL LETTER TO THE MIND HUSTLER

If you could write a letter to The Mind Hustler, what would you say?

_____
_____
_____
_____
_____
_____
_____
_____
_____
_____
_____

"The true power of a seed is that everything it hopes to become is already inside; what all seeds need is a help getting into the ground."

THE POWER OF ONE

Think about a person who was there for you at a trying moment in your life and the person dropped wisdom on you and/or encouraged you. You now have the opportunity to write the person a thank you note and update him or her where you are in life. Include your dreams, hopes and aspirations.

_____
_____
_____
_____
_____
_____
_____
_____
_____
_____
_____

BEWARE THE MIND HUSTLER: IDENTIFYING SELF-DESTRUCTIVE THOUGHTS AND DISTRACTIONS

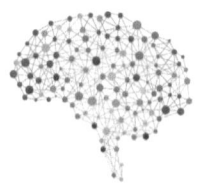

"You may be locked up but that does not mean you are locked out."

THE LAST WORD:
HOW I ESCAPED THE MIND HUSTLER
~ VIVIAN D. NIXON

In 1998, I was leading a bible study at Albion Correctional Facility. I was teaching a lesson I had learned earlier from Rev. Alfonso Wyatt when he came to the small Long Island church I attended in my youth. The lesson was Gideon's Army and it instilled in me the faith that power is not in numbers; power is resisting The Mind Hustler's whispers of doubt that make us believe that a task is insurmountable. The oxymoron in this particular prison bible study is that I was not only the teacher, I was a woman who had a New York State Correction Department Identification Number (DIN): Nixon 98G0357. I was wearing greens. I was an incarcerated woman. I entered the ministry *before* becoming what insiders call "state property." When detectives visited me at my place of employment in 1997, it hit me like a ton of bricks when I was charged, prosecuted, and sentenced to prison for things I had done three years earlier. The details of my past crimes are not important in the context of my thoughts about this book. What is important is how I escaped The Mind Hustler.

Whether it was pure happenstance or divine intervention

just days before I was released someone handed me a brochure worded do you want to go to college? I did, so College and Community Fellowship (CCF) was the first number I dialed once on the outside. I became one of the first fellows in this fledgling program designed to help formerly incarcerated women by supporting them as they pursue college degrees. I am currently Executive Director of CCF and we continue to enable women with criminal convictions to earn their college degrees so that they, their families and their communities can thrive and advocate for equity and opportunity for the communities we serve. When I first joined CCF after prison in 2001, it was the only organization that focused on elevating the strength of the mind as a way to navigate successfully despite systemic, structural, and spiritual hurdles.

As a CCF Fellow, I earned a Bachelor of Science Degree in Human Services Management from the State University of New York. But, the most life-changing experience I had was the time I spent as a peer educator in the adult basic education and a leader in the chapel bible study circle in state prison. When I graduated in 2006, I intended to go straight to graduate school. However, outside interest in CCF increased and the scope of the work began to grow rapidly. I now oversee multiple direct service programs, a national public policy coalition, technical assistance program and a staff of twenty. The years from 2006-2017 were consumed managing the growth of the organization. I postponed healthcare; I postponed my dreams of graduate school; I neglected friends, family and fellowship. The harsh reality is this: In doing so, I was mind-hustled into believing that my worth was tied to the work instead of embracing the fact I had been divinely anointed and appointed for a time and still had a right to pursue personal fulfillment apart from the work.

CCF was created to fight a battle that no other organization at the time was fighting—the battle to infuse the minds of formerly incarcerated women with confidence in their power and their abilities so that they would not be hustled by people or systems that might keep them from reaching their full potential. I decided to flip the script on The Mind Hustler and follow the advice of the organization I was leading. Running the organization could no longer come before my health and personal development. In 2017, I returned to graduate school to pursue a life-long dream. In May 2019, I will finish my coursework at Columbia University School of The Arts. May 2020, upon approval of my thesis, I will receive a Master's Degree in Fine Arts. Has all of this caused me to learn to say *no* to twenty-four-seven availability to CCF (an organization that I love)? Yes. Has this required some staying home some Sundays to write a paper rather that attend church? Yes. Has this required turning down speaking engagements or requests to mentor others while I work on my personal goals? Yes. It was hard to avoid The Mind Hustler's comments like, "If you were really about social justice you would..." If you were really a Christian you would..." I refused to be hustled.

The creator gives each of us a unique set of skills, gifts, and talents. The world will often send messages that appear to come from allies but they are really coming from the camp of our mental adversary. The Mind Hustler is tricky using artifices and deceits that make self-sabotaging ideas seem like a good thing. Know that even a good suggestion can be an interruption of your journey toward the thing that you are truly called to do. There are many virtuous things needed in this world. Don't be hustled into thinking you have to do them all. Do what the creator has put you on the planet to do. Never permit The Mind Hustler to persuade you that you must have sycophantic devotion to every whim and ideology is the healthy way to survive. The creator has more than survival in mind for you—the creator wants you to thrive! Remember, your gifts will make room for you, especially if you are resolved to evict The Mind Hustler.

> *The Reverend Vivian D. Nixon is Executive Director of College & Community Fellowship. As a formerly incarcerated woman and CCF program graduate, Rev. Nixon is uniquely positioned to lead the movement to ensure that justice-involved women and their families have a better future. While incarcerated, Rev. Nixon spent time as a peer educator for the adult basic education program at Albion State Correctional Facility in New York. During 3 ½ years in prison, Vivian gained clarity about the correlation between access to education and incarceration. She describes her most formative experience as tutoring fellow incarcerated women. In prison, Vivian began to formulate her own ideas about the ways that the criminal justice system disproportionately burdens women. Upon release in 2001, Vivian finished her college degree as a client of CCF, and began applying her perspective to the emerging discourse about criminal justice reform.*

Vivian earned her B.S. with CCF's help and was appointed its Executive Director in 2006. She is a Columbia University Community Scholar and a recipient of the John Jay Medal for Justice, the Ascend Fellowship at the Aspen Institute, the Soros Justice Fellowship, and the Petra Foundation Fellowship. She is a 2017 honoree of the New York Women's Foundation & Tribeca Disruptive Innovator Awards, and appeared on New York Nonprofit Media's 2018 50 Over 50 list. She is the Board Chair of JustLeadershipUSA, a nonprofit that empowers those most affected by incarceration to drive policy reform. Currently, Rev. Nixon serves on the Close Rikers design team.

Vivian's work has changed the conversation around higher education in criminal justice reform. Never content to accept that subsistence living equals reentry success, Vivian has dedicated her personal time and resources to ensuring that major players in the movement – from activists and service providers to philanthropists and policymakers – understand that people with justice histories are still people: they have dreams, skills, and strengths, and are capable of more than minimum-wage jobs.

Rev. Nixon holds a Bachelor of Science degree from the State University of New York Empire State College, and is currently an MFA candidate in creative nonfiction at Columbia University. She will also be a Columbia Teaching Fellow in the MFA program for the school year 2019-20.

PART IV

Suggested Reading: Authors Who Escaped From The Belly Of The Beast

PART IV : SUGGESTED READINGS

Bartlett, Elaine, and Jennifer Gonnerman. *Life On The Outside The Prison Odyssey of Elaine Bartlett.*

Benjamin, J.M., and Randy Kearse. *From Incarceration 2 Incorporation.*

Boothe, Demico. *Getting Out & Staying Out: A Black Man's Guide to Success After Prison.*

Bovan, Richard. *The Dedicated Ex-Prisoner's Guide to Life an Success on the Outside: 10 Rules for Making It in Society After Doing Time.*

Brooks, G. S. *The Psychology of Freedom.*

Brown, Harvey. *Freedom at Last: The Life of an Ex-Con.*

Ferguson, Darren A. *How I Became an Angry Black Man: From Prison to the Pulpit.*

Flores, F. Mateen. *Pass Da 'El.*

Hinton, Anthony Ray, and Lara Love Hardin. *The Sun Does Shine How I Found Life And Freedom On Death Row.*

Hylton, Donna. *A Little Piece of Light: A Memoir of Hope, Prison and a Life Unbound.*

Jackson, Michael B. *How To Do Good After Prison: A Handbook for Successful Reentry (W/Employment Information Handbook).*

Kearse, Randy. *Changin' Your Game Plan! How to use incarceration* as a stepping stone for success.

Kearse, Randy. *From Prison to Prosperity: The Randy Kearse Story*.

Robinson, Joseph. *Think Outside the Cell: An Entrepreneur's Guide for the Incarcerated and Formerly Incarcerated*.

Shird, Kevin. *Lessons of Redemption #DoRight*

Waters, Easy. *Streets of Rage*.

Waters, William E. *Black Shadows and Through the White Looking Glass: Remembrance of Things Past and Present*.

Waters, William E. *Sometimes Blue Knights Wear Black Hats*.

ADDITIONAL MIND FORTIFYING READING

Alexander, Michelle. *The New Jim Crow: Mass Incarceration in the Age of Colorblindness*.

Blake, W. Bessie. *God's Bad Boy: James Blake & The System*.

Davis, Askia Akhenaton Suleiman Ali, and Askia Davis Sr. Ed.D. *Coming of Age in the Hip Hop Generation: Warrior of the Void*.

Egers, Edith Eva. *The Choice: Embrace The Impossible*

Fox, Butterfield. *All God's Children; The Bosket Family and America's Tradition of Violence*.

PART IV : SUGGESTED READINGS

Germaine, Jim, St., Jon Sternfeld. *A Stone of Hope A Memoir.*

Hefner, Keith, and Laura Longhine. *A Leader's Guide to Real Men: Urban Teens Write About How to Be a Man.*

Krebs, Betsy, and Paul Pitcoff. *Beyond the Foster Care System: The Future of Teens.*

Moore, Wes. *The Other Wes Moore: One Name, Two Fates*

Robertson, Howard. *The 411 On Bullying, Gangs, Drugs and Jail The Formula For Staying In School And Out Of Jail.*

Stevenson, Bryan. *Just Mercy.*

Toure. *Who's Afraid of Post-Blackness? What It Means To Be Black Now.*

Travis, Jeremy. *But They All Come Home: Facing the Challenge of Prisoner Reentry.*

Webber, L. Thomas. *Flying Over 96th Street: Memoir of an East Harlem White Boy.*

Wilson, Jason, and Eshon Burgundy. *Cry Like A Man: Fighting for Freedom From Emotional Incarceration*

Westbrook, Peter. *Harnessing Anger: The Way Of An American Fencer*

White, Khary Lazarre. *Passage*

Wyatt, Alfonso. *Madd Truth: Lasting Lessons for Students of Life.*

Wyatt, Alfonso. *Mentoring From The Inside Out: Healing Boys Transforming Men.*

Wyatt, Alfonso, and Ouida Wyatt. *Before You Jump The Broom Clean Up Your Room.*

Wyatt, Alfonso, and Ouida Wyatt. *Soul Be Free Poems Prose Prayers.*

Wyatt, Alfonso, and Ouida Wyatt. *Soul Be Free II.*

Wyatt, Alfonso, and Ouida Wyatt. *Soul Be Free III: Different Hues of The Blues.*

PART V

Wisdom Sayings To Repel The Mind Hustler

PART V : COMPILATION OF WISDOM SAYINGS

1. "You are given free will at birth to become anything that you want to be in life; it is your responsibility to choose wisely."

2. "There can never be lasting external change without the intentional internal death of harmful dysfunctional thought patterns."

3. "A troubled mind can make enemies friends, or make friends enemies. A troubled mind can bring short-lived comfort, or long-term torment."

4. "When you have time to rummage through your mind, be careful to not over refine those thoughts not yet properly defined."

5. "If you find people to blame for your circumstance you will never be free because the only person who can change your condition is you."

6. "When breaking bread with trusted friends the question is why would you allow fear a seat at the table?"

7. "Mind Games Defined: Player is too invested in the game to quit and too tired to proceed; are you stuck playing games that cannot be won?"

8. "When the desire to know self overtake the lack of self-knowledge, this glorious event marks the birth of insight."

9. "Know the mind can travel effortlessly back and forth to the past, present, or future but the body can only exist in the right now."

10. "Make this part of your mantra: I will no longer go on trips that

I didn't pack the suitcases for."

11. "I fought thoughts of fear, doubt, anger and discovered I was the boss of my mind. This revolutionary 'mind-find' freed me from me."

12. "Light can create shadows; the same light can eradicate shadows—this contradiction must be reconciled in order to grow and thrive."

13. "The dualistic power of hope can kindle a deep desire to persevere in the face of overwhelming obstacles while inspiring others to do the same."

14. "There can never be lasting external change without the intentional internal death of harmful dysfunctional habits and thought patterns."

15. "Hustling Backwards Defined: Taking two steps up and three steps back yet never thinking you owe a step just to get back to where you started."

16. "If you want something of value out of life that you don't presently have, you must be willing to put in valuable time in order to get it."

17. "If you don't build your own dreams, someone will hire you to build theirs." (Quote offered by contributor)

18. "The only thing that can defeat hope happens when one loses faith in hope."

19. "The dualistic power of hope can kindle a deep desire to per-

severe in the face of adversity while inspiring others to do the same."

20. "Some people have self-sentenced themselves to do voluntary solitary confinement in the dungeon of sad yesterday."

21. "Please do not be tricked, no matter who you are or where you come from, you must always remember—there is no future in the past."

22. "Once you find your mission in life, take what was designed to destroy you and you destroy it."

23. "Running from the truth is a race that will never be won no matter how fast you run."

24. "Don't think just because you want to do right that your mind will automatically agree to help you get right."

25. "In order to see, you first must look; know this, just because you look does not automatically mean you will see."

26. "There can never be lasting external change without the intentional death of harmful dysfunctional internal thought patterns."

27. "People going through life troubles must know it is important to name their inner adversary because you cannot defeat what you cannot name."

28. "A very important life lesson is never see personal weakness or setbacks as a reason to throw in the towel as oppose to an opportunity to grow."

29. "A person's outer glow is in proportion to their inner glow. The more a person glows on the inside, the brighter the glow on the outside."

30. "A person with larceny in their heart is hard to help because they view the intentions of people through the lens of a hustler, thus mischaracterizing some people who genuinely want to help."

31. "Who is the real you inside of you? If you don't know, or perhaps forgotten, go inside yourself and look for the real you so you can let go of the manufactured broken image created by the old you."

32. "God save me from my friends; I can handle my enemies." (Unknown)

33. "Some people confuse having a desire to change with actually changing. If there is no executed plan of action then desire becomes its own reward."

34. "When the desire to know self overtakes ignorance of self know this glorious moment marks the birth of insight."

35. "There are truths residing deep in the heart waiting for the day of liberation."

36. "The true power of a seed is that everything it hopes to become is already inside; what all seeds need is a help getting into the ground."

37. "You may be locked up but that does not mean you are locked out."

GONE, BUT NOT FORGOTTEN:

Eddie Ellis

Lonnie McLeod

Bill Webber

OTHER BOOKS BY DR. ALFONSO WYATT

Dr. Alfonso Wyatt's books are available through all major online book retailers or through Strategic Destiny: @alfonsowyatt09@gmail.com.

www.ingramcontent.com/pod-product-compliance
Lightning Source LLC
Chambersburg PA
CBHW030437010526
44118CB00011B/673